To Marisa, for making sure I don't do all my socializing via the Internet.

About the Author

Scott McNulty has been known to Google himself from time to time. He is also an unabashed early adopter and technology enthusiast, with an undeniable urge to share his excitement about technology with the world.

Scott lives in Philadelphia with his wife, Marisa. By day he works at the The Wharton School of the University of Pennsylvania, and by night he blogs about whatever strikes his fancy at http://blog.blankbaby.com. He has also been known to tweet once or twice under the handle @blankbaby.

Acknowledgments

Once again, I'm thankful to all the talented people without whom this book would not exist. Cliff Colby talked me into writing the book, and I thank him for that. Kathy Simpson once again had the unenviable task of taking my scribblings and making them human-readable, and she did a stellar job, as always. Thanks to Maureen Forys, Kim Wimpsett, and Mimi Heft, who made this book look as great as it does. And thanks to Valerie Haynes Perry for indexing the heck out of it.

This book was a team effort; any errors in the text, however, are mine alone.

Contents

Introduction

Google+ is the newest kid on the social-networking block—a service that allows you to post your thoughts, photos, videos, and more to your stream (see Chapter 1). People who follow you on Google+ can see what you've posted on your stream and share it with their followers.

Now, you may be thinking, "I thought we had enough social networks to keep up with already: Twitter, Facebook, even MySpace. Why add another?" That's a very good question, and I'm sure that many smart people at Google asked the same question before they launched Google+. How can I be so sure? Because it all that careful thought shows when you're using Google+.

What Google+ Offers

Google+ offers a bevy of features that allow you to share different things with different people. That final bit is the interesting part: Google+ makes it downright simple to share particular things with only certain people.

I clearly remember the day when Facebook changed for me forever: A friend request from my mother appeared in my inbox. Now, I love my mother, and I couldn't refuse to be her friend (that might have resulted in some awkward Thanksgiving meals), but when your mom is your friend on Facebook, that fact affects the way you use the service. The same can be said when your boss and co-workers friend you on Facebook.

Facebook is invested in your sharing things with the widest audience possible, as the default privacy settings reflect. Lately, Facebook has gotten better about allowing you to choose who can see what, but Google+ was designed with choice in mind. Google+ is the first social network to embrace the idea that people have several groups of people in their lives: relatives, friends, co-workers, the Tuesday-night poker group, and so on. The list is incredibly different from person to person. Isn't it odd, then, that most social networks assume that you want to share the same things across all those groups? Google+ doesn't.

In the following sections, I take a quick look at the features this book covers to give you an idea of what Google+ has to offer.

Circles

The cornerstone of your Google+ experience is circles, which group people in your Google+ network. You can share whatever you post to Google+ with any number of your circles, and you can create your own custom circles.

Google+ also has some default circles:

- Friends
- Family
- Acquaintances
- Following

I dive into circles in Chapter 2.

Hangouts

Google+ makes sharing things with other folks on Google+ easy. It makes talking to them very easy as well. You can start a video conference call, or hangout, by clicking a button. Better yet, you can invite people from any of your circles to join you in your hangout. If you aren't into the idea of video/audio conferencing, hangouts also support group chat so that you can type your thoughts.

Hangouts, and some uses for them, are covered in Chapter 4.

Messenger

The builders of any new social network would be crazy to ignore the explosive growth of mobile devices, so Google+ has a couple of features that are designed to be used only with mobile devices. Messenger, the most prominent of the mobile-only features, is a text-messaging service of sorts—without the fees.

You can message with anyone in your circles. As long as both you and your contact have the Google+ app on your devices (iOS or Android), you can send text and pictures to each other.

I cover this feature in Chapter 7.

Pictures

Google+ allows you to share that funny cat picture you found on the Internet. It's also become something of a go-to service where photographers can show off their work to their peers and get feedback, thanks to Google+'s robust commenting and 1+ system (the Google+ analogue to Facebook's Like).

You can not only share individual pictures, but also create entire albums of photos and share them with any and all of your circles. Only the people with whom you've shared the photos can comment on them.

Creating, sharing, and managing photo albums on Google+ are covered in Chapter 5.

The rest

The preceding four features would make a pretty good social network all by themselves, but Google didn't stop there. Here are some more features that aren't integral to the Google+ experience at the moment but that have growth potential:

- **Search.** Search is fully baked into Google+, allowing you to search for people, posts, sparks, or other interesting things to post. Chapter 6 is all about search.

- **Location.** In addition to sharing video, text, images, or links with people on Google+, you can share your physical location. See Chapter 3 for details.

- **Instant Upload.** If you have an Android device running Android 2.1 or later, and you install the Google+ app, you can take advantage of Instant Upload. After this feature is set up, all the images you take on your Android device are uploaded to Google+ but kept in a private album until you decide to share them. I cover the ins and outs of Instant Upload in Chapter 5.

- **Games.** Yes, you can play Angry Birds in Google+. What more do you need to know? Chapter 8 covers accessing games and sharing scores (and also tells you why Google+ games aren't as annoying as Facebook games).

Updates for This Book

One of the most challenging things about being a tech-book author is the rapid pace of technological change. I type as fast as my fingers let me, yet the technology changes even faster. Google+ is a prime example. Google, the company, thinks of Google+ as a project, and it's actively developing this project, adding tweaks, changes, and new features at a pretty steady rate.

With all these unknown future features, won't this book become out of date? No, because when you buy it, you aren't buying just the book: You're also buying four updates that cover whatever big features Google adds to Google+.

Because I don't have access to Google's internal plans for rolling out features, it's impossible to predict when the updates will be available. Make sure that you register your copy of this book at www.peachpit.com/googleplusguide to get your free updates.

One of the biggest features missing at the moment, for example, is business profiles. Google+ is all about individual users, but lots of companies are very eager to hold "conversations" with consumers who use Google+. (In other words, they want to use Google+ to sell you things. Commerce isn't always bad, though.) Shortly after Google adds this feature to Google+, Peachpit Press will provide an update to this book that explains how to use business profiles. Neat, huh?

Getting Started with Google+

The Google+ project is open to public signups now, so if you go to http://plus.google.com, you'll see a nice Web page with a big red Sign In button. All you need to sign up for Google+ are a Google account and a desire to share interesting things with people.

This chapter covers how to get yourself a Google account (if you already have one, feel free to skip that section), set up your Google+ profile, and find some interesting people to follow.

Getting a Google Account

You may have a Google account and not even know it. If you use Google services like Gmail or Picasa, you already have a Google account. You can use the same login information for Google+, so feel free to skip this section and go straight to "Creating a public profile."

If you don't use any Google services, you need to get yourself a Google account. Luckily, the process is pretty easy.

Because this book is about Google+, you may as well set up your new account via the Google+ home page. Here's what you do:

1. Point your browser of choice to http://plus.google.com (**Figure 1.1**).

2. Click the Create an Account link below the Sign In button (**Figure 1.2**).

3. Fill in all the information that the form requires, making sure to enter a strong password.

4. Click the button labeled I Accept. Create My Account.

Your Google account has been created, and you're taken to the Google+ profile-creation page (see the next section).

Figure 1.2 The Google+ login page accepts only Google accounts.

Creating a public profile

If you already have or just created a Google account, now you need to set up your Google+ profile (which will also be your Google profile).

Registering your Google+ name

After you've signed up or logged in, the profile page opens (**Figure 1.3**).

Figure 1.3 Create a Google+ profile here.

In the profile box, you must enter your first and last names and your gender. You can also add an optional profile picture, as I explain in the next section.

 All users are required to register under their legal names, not under wacky nicknames (which is why I'm not known as blankbaby on Google+).

Uploading a profile photo

Your profile picture accompanies pretty much everything you post to Google+, so make sure that you choose a good one. It's probably a good idea to use a picture of yourself, though that's not required.

To upload a profile picture, follow these steps:

1. Click the Change Photo link in the profile box (refer to Figure 1.3).

The photo uploader appears (**Figure 1.4**).

Figure 1.4 You can drag a profile photo into the box.

2. Drag a photo into the photo uploader, or click the Select a Photo from Your Computer button to locate and upload a photo from your computer.

3. Crop the picture so that it will display correctly (**Figure 1.5**).

The box represents the section of the photo that will appear in your Google+ profile, so drag it onto the section of the photo you want to display. You can rotate the photo by clicking the rotation icons near the top-right corner.

Figure 1.5 Make sure that your profile picture shows your face.

Click to rotate counterclockwise.

Click to rotate clockwise.

Drag this box to crop the photo.

 Even more photo-editing options are available to you if you click the Edit Photo in Picnik link. Picnik (www.picnik.com) is a browser-based application that can do lots of basic photo-editing tasks.

4. When you're happy with the image, click the Set As Profile Photo button.

 If you have a webcam and Adobe Flash on your computer, you can even snap a picture and set that as your profile picture. Just click the Web Camera option in the photo uploader (refer to Figure 1.4).

Providing personal info

After you set a profile picture, click the red Join button. A new page appears, giving you the opportunity to provide more info about yourself (**Figure 1.6**). Listing your school and year of graduation, along with where you work and live, makes it easier for people to figure out whether you're the guy they went to school with or some other dude.

Figure 1.6 Google wants you to add as much information as possible to your profile so that people can find you on Google+.

Add additional profile information to your public profile.
Adding more information will help your friends, family, and others find and connect with you.

School	School name	Year
Where you work	Employer	Job title
Where you live	Enter a city or a country	

Profile basics

Help your friends find you and find more people you went to school with, work with, or once lived nearby.

Upload a photo from your computer or take a picture with your webcam.

Change profile photo

When you start typing a school or employer name, Google tries to guess what you're typing and makes suggestions based on what other users have entered (**Figure 1.7**).

Figure 1.7 Many fields attempt to autopopulate with common values. Go, Lehigh!

Click Continue when you're done.

Adding contacts

The next page lets you add contacts from any Yahoo Mail or Hotmail email accounts you may have (**Figure 1.8**). Just click the Yahoo or Hotmail icon and then log in to your email account with the proper credentials. Google searches the account's address book and presents a list of contacts you can add to Google+ (see Chapter 2). If you don't use either of those services, click the Skip button at the bottom of the page.

Figure 1.8 Google can search your Yahoo or Hotmail address book for people who are already on Google+.

Finding company

Finally, Google+ is a lonely place when you aren't following anyone, so in the last setup page, Google suggests some famous and/or interesting people you may be interested in following on Google+ (**Figure 1.9**). Google recommends that you follow at least ten of these people to make your stream interesting, but I leave the number of famous people you want to follow on Google+ up to you.

These people are grouped in sections, such as Picks, Entertainment, and Music. Clicking one of the sections displays the users contained therein.

Figure 1.9 Google suggests some people you may be interested in following on Google+.

If you find someone that you'd like to follow on Google+, just click the Add to Circles button next to his or her photo, and you can add that person to any of the default circles (**Figure 1.10**). Don't worry about what circles are at the moment; I cover them in Chapter 2.

Figure 1.10 Click the Add to Circles button to add a person to one of your default circles.

When you're done, click the blue Continue button at the bottom of the page. You're taken to your Google+ Stream, which is where most of the action happens in Google+.

Touring the Google+ Stream

Now that you have a Google+ account, a quick tour of the stream interface (**Figure 1.11**, on the next page) is in order. I expand on each of these concepts in later chapters.

Plus bar ——
Google+ toolbar ——

Figure 1.11 This is what your stream will look like when you start putting people in your circles.

Plus bar

At the top of the page is the black Plus bar, which shows up on all Google pages as long as you're logged in and allows you to switch among various Google services. The first link goes to Google+. The Plus bar also displays Google+ notifications in red (I have one in Figure 1.11), the Share box (more on that in Chapter 2), and your profile picture. If you click your profile picture, you get a few options (**Figure 1.12**).

Figure 1.12 The Plus bar gives you a few options when you click the small profile image.

Google+ toolbar

Below the Plus bar, you'll find the Google+ toolbar. Next to the Google+ logo are icons for the different aspects of your Google+ account (**Figure 1.13**): Home (also known as the stream; see Chapter 3), Photos (see Chapter 5), Profile (see "Editing Your Profile Page" later in this chapter), Circles (see Chapter 2), and Games (see Chapter 8).

Figure 1.13 The Google+ toolbar is home to all the Google+ tabs.

Right next to the navigation icons is the search box, which I cover in "Finding People to Follow" at the end of this chapter.

Personal information

Your profile picture and name appear at the top of the leftmost column, which includes the following items:

- **A Welcome link.** Click this link to read some information about Google+.
- **Stream list.** You can view each of your circle's streams individually or see everything in one place. Clicking a circle's name shows only items from the members of that circle in your stream. Clicking Stream shows all the people you follow in one stream. This list includes a special circle called Incoming, which I mention in the next section and explain fully in Chapter 3.
- **Saved-searches list.** You can save your Google+ searches for one-click access. Chapter 6 shows you how to do this.
- **Chat list.** If you have one, your Gtalk contact list is integrated with Google+. Check out www.google.com/talk for more information about Gtalk.

Stream lists

The middle column is all about the stream, offering the following elements (**Figure 1.14**):

- **Share box.** This box is where sharing starts. Whether you want to share a message, a video, or an image, you do it here. For more on sharing, flip to Chapter 3.

Figure 1.14 The Google+ Stream is where you'll spend most of your time.

- **Incoming section.** People can share things with you on Google+, and if you don't follow them back, they show up in the Incoming section of the stream. The most recent additions to the Incoming group are displayed here.

- **The stream.** The stream itself displays everything you've shared and whatever the folks in your circles are sharing with you and/or the world.

Networking details

The right column displays the following:

- **In Your Circles section.** Click the View All link to see all the people in your circles.

- **Suggestions list.** Here, Google+ lists people you may want to add to your circles.

- **Invitations section.** Even though Google+ is now open to all, you can still send invitations to your friends, encouraging them to join in on the fun. Click the Invite Friends button to invite other people to Google+. Above this button, you see the number of invitations you have left. (Every Google+ user can issue 150 invitations.)

- **Hangouts section.** You can start a hangout—basically, a video/audio conference—by clicking the green Start a Hangout button. I explore hangouts in Chapter 4.

Editing Your Profile Page

Now that you can find your way around Google+, you really should take a moment to fill in as much profile information as you're comfortable sharing. This information helps people be sure they're following the person they want to follow and allows them to find you on the service more easily.

You have several ways to get to your Google+ profile:

- If you're logged in to Google+, just go to https://plus.google.com/me.
- Click the Profile icon ⊙ on the Google+ toolbar.
- Click your profile picture in the left column.
- Click your profile picture on the Plus bar and then click the Profile link.

No matter which method you use, you're taken to your profile page (**Figure 1.15**). This page has six tabs: Posts, About, Photos, Videos, +1's, and Buzz. With the exception of About, each tab lists all the content of that type that you've posted on Google+.

Figure 1.15 The profile page lists information about you.

The About tab lists all the profile information you've entered about yourself in Google+. Click it to see what you have listed. **Figure 1.16** shows my profile page, and as you see, I've filled in a good bit of profile information.

Figure 1.16 The About tab of your profile page contains information that describes you.

What if you want to change something or add more details? The good news is that almost everything you see on your profile page can be edited. Click the blue Edit Profile button to add or subtract information and to change who can see it (**Figure 1.17**). When you click that button, you see the options available for each section. In the following sections, I discuss these options, starting with the left column and working my way right.

Figure 1.17 All the fields on the About tab are editable.

Privacy Settings

Every bit of editable content on your profile page also has its very own privacy setting. You can choose who can or can't see the information, and you can do so in a very granular way.

When you're editing a section, a drop-down menu at the bottom lists different levels of privacy (**Figure 1.18**).

Figure 1.18 The profile privacy options for each individual section of your profile.

(continued)

The options include

- **Anyone on the Web.** This option is the most open one, making your information totally public.

- **Extended Circles.** Whatever has this privacy setting can be viewed by the people in your circles and anyone in their circles. Suppose that John is in one of your circles, and Ken is in John's circle but not yours. If you apply the Extended Circles setting to your email link, Ken would be able to see it even though he's not in one of your circles.

- **Your Circles.** This setting limits the information to people you've placed in a circle of your own.

- **Only You.** You're the only person who can see this information—and only when you're logged in to Google+.

- **Custom.** Custom gives you total control over who can see this piece of information. Want to limit your email to be visible only to one circle or just one person? Custom lets you do that.

Left column

The left column of Google+ is all about you. Your profile picture is listed there, along with your circles, your saved searches, and your Gtalk contacts (if you have any).

Profile Picture

You can change your profile photo in this section. To delete your current photo, click the white X in its top-right corner (refer to Figure 1.17); then click the Change Photo link to upload another profile picture. The process is the same as described in "Uploading a profile photo" earlier in this chapter.

Send an Email

Clicking the Send an Email section opens a pane that allows you to determine who can, or can't, send you an email via your Google+ profile (**Figure 1.19**, on the next page). If you want people to be able to send you email, check the box titled Allow People to Email You from a Link on Your Profile. (By default, this box is unchecked.) You can also set your privacy levels; see the nearby "Privacy Settings" sidebar for details.

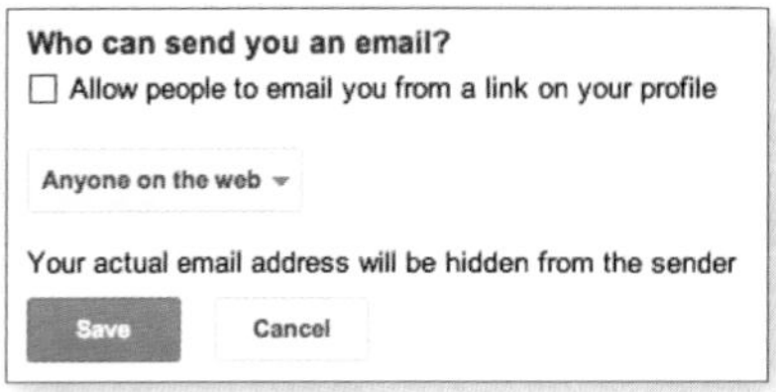

Figure 1.19 Email privacy settings make sure that you don't get unwanted email.

When you finish, click the Save button to save your changes.

Circles

Circles are covered fully in Chapter 2, but by now, you've picked up on the fact that they're groups of people. Your profile has a circle-related display right below your profile picture. That grid of other people's profile pictures represents two things: the people in your circles at the top and people who have you in their circles at the bottom (**Figure 1.20**).

By default, your profile page displays grids of people in your circles and people who have you in their circles. To change this display, click the grid itself or the Change Who Is Visible Here link. You can display only people from certain circles in your profile and also turn off the option to display people who have you in their circles (**Figure 1.21**).

Figure 1.20 (near right) People in your circles, and who have circled you, are displayed on your profile page by default.

Figure 1.21 (far right) You can choose whether you want your profile page to display the people who are in your circles and the people who list you in their circles.

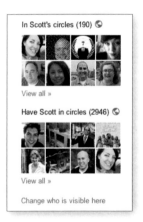

Center column

Moving on to the center column, I'll start at the top and work down.

 Each of these editable regions includes the privacy settings described in the "Privacy Settings" sidebar earlier in this chapter.

Name

Yep, you can change your name in Google+ just by clicking it while you're editing your profile page and then typing a new name (**Figure 1.22**). Click the Save button when you're done. This change affects your name on all the services that you access with this Google account, including Gmail.

Figure 1.22 Change your name by retyping it here.

 Keep in mind that Google really sticks to its "real name" policy. It audits profiles and suspends any profiles whose owners may be using fake names, so don't try.

Tagline

Click the tagline below your name (refer to Figure 1.17) to change it to something else.

Photos

You can add photos to your profile by clicking the Add Some Photos Here link (refer to Figure 1.17) and uploading some images. The photos will appear on your profile page but won't replace your profile picture (**Figure 1.23**, on the next page).

Figure 1.23 Additional photos spruce up your profile page.

Figure 1.23 Additional photos spruce up your profile page.

Introduction

Your introduction can be much longer than your tagline. Write a paragraph or two describing who you are, and don't be afraid to get a little creative!

Bragging Rights

This section always strikes me as being as odd, as it's straightforward: List things that you brag about. Perhaps you can hold your breath for a really long time, or maybe you own every Kindle model ever made. Either factoid, or both, would be great in the Bragging Rights section of your Google+ profile. (Only one of those things is true of me, by the way. Can you guess which?)

Occupation, Employment, and Education

I'm grouping these items because they go together and are self-explanatory. When you're entering your company or school's name, Google suggests existing names based on what other people have already entered, to save you some typing.

Places Lived

One of the first questions people ask when they meet someone new is "Where are you from?" This section of your profile page (**Figure 1.24**) asks that same question. You can list as many places as you've lived; just enter their names and click Save. When you're done, a map showing all the places you've listed is included in your Google+ profile (**Figure 1.25**).

Figure 1.24 List all the places that you've called home.

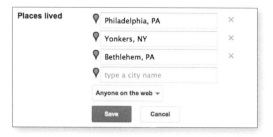

Figure 1.25 Google+ plots your Places Lived entries on a map that's displayed on your profile page.

Home/Work

Want people to know your home phone number or your work email address? List them here. Be sure to set the privacy settings to include just the people you want to have accessing this information.

Relationship

Just as you can on Facebook, you can list what kind of relationship you're in. I'm married (sorry, ladies), so I chose the Married option. Other options include I Don't Want to Say and In a Civil Union.

Looking For

This section (**Figure 1.26**) lets people know why you're on Google+. You can choose any combination of Friends, Dating, A Relationship, or Networking. Just check the boxes next to the items you're interested in. Set the privacy level (I've picked Extended Circles in Figure 1.26), and click Save.

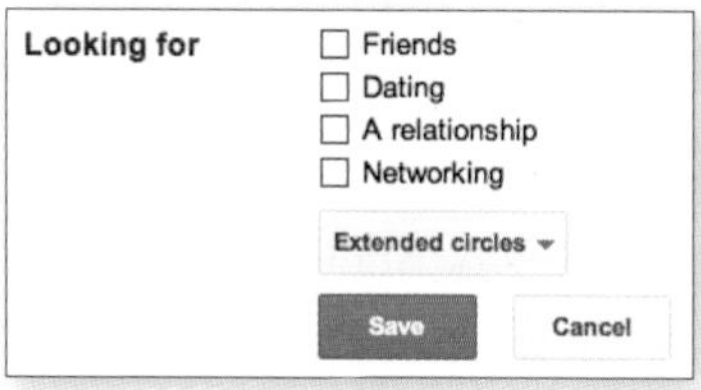

Figure 1.26 If you're looking for love on Google+, make sure that people know!

Gender

The options in this section are Male, Female, and Other.

Other Names

This text box that allows you to enter your maiden name or an alternative spelling of your name.

Nickname

Blankbaby is my nickname (on the Internet), so I added it to my profile in this section.

Search Visibility

In addition to making Google+, Google offers a search engine. By default, your Google+ profile is indexed by search engines, meaning that people who are searching for your name may find your Google+ profile in their results. If you don't want your profile to be indexed in Google search results, you can change that setting in the Search Visibility section (**Figure 1.27**). Clear the check box titled Help Others Find My Profile in Search Results, and click Save.

Figure 1.27 By default, all Google+ profiles are indexed by search engines, so people can view and find them without being logged in to Google+.

Links

As you might expect, the links on your Google+ profile page point to other you-related places on the Internet. The links are separated into three groups:

- **Other Profiles.** Other Profiles is where you should list your profiles on other Web sites (Twitter, Facebook, and the like).

- **Contributor To.** Contributor To is great for the writers and photographers out there, because you can list all the places where your work is featured.

- **Recommended Links.** Recommended Links is the place for semirandom links that you want to be associate with your profile.

To edit any section, click it. **Figure 1.28** shows the form that appears when you click Other Profiles (with your own profiles listed, of course). To edit a link, click the blue pencil icon next to it. The resulting form (**Figure 1.29**) allows you to change the URL of the link as well as its descriptive text.

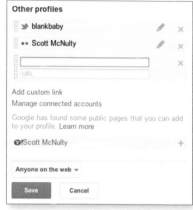

Figure 1.28 (near right) Add links to your other Internet profiles here by using a custom link or connecting an account to your Google+ profile.

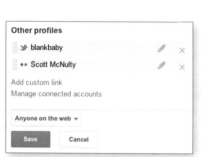

Figure 1.29 (far right) A link consists of a name and a URL.

You can add two types of links in the Other Profiles section: custom links and connected accounts.

Custom links

Custom links can point to anything on the Internet. To add one, click Add Custom Link in the Links section (refer to Figure 1.28), and enter the name of the link and the URL.

Connected accounts

Clicking the Manage Connected Accounts link (refer to Figure 1.28) actually takes you to the Google+ Connected Accounts Web page (**Figure 1.30**). The accounts that appear here show up on your Google+ profile page as links.

Figure 1.30 Connecting external accounts to your Google account allows Google to access information about those accounts.

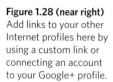

The accounts that you can connect are Facebook, Yahoo, Flickr, LinkedIn, Quora, Twitter, Yelp, Hotmail, MySpace, and Plaxo. To connect one of those accounts, click the Connect an Account button, and choose it from the pop-up menu. Depending on which account you choose, either a text box or a pop-up window opens. If you get a text box (**Figure 1.31**), enter a URL and click the green Add button; if you get a pop-up window, log in to that account to connect it.

Figure 1.31 Fill in your Facebook profile's URL to connect it to your Google account.

 When you're adding a URL with the text box, you have the option to add the link to your public Google profile. Be aware that this link will be available to anyone who finds your profile.

To remove a link, just click the Remove button next to it.

Finding People to Follow

Your profile is all set up, helping people find you on Google+. But how do you find people yourself? Using Google+ without following people isn't much fun unless you really like talking to yourself. Luckily, you have three main ways to find people on Google+: searching Google+, searching for public Google+ profiles via Google search, and using some new directory Web sites that exist for just this purpose. In this section, I cover all three methods.

Doing a native Google+ search

Right at the top of every Google+ page is a search box labeled Search Google+ (**Figure 1.32**). To use it, just start typing the name of someone you're looking for in Google+.

Figure 1.32 The Search Google+ box is just waiting for you to enter someone's name in it.

To search for someone in Google+, follow these steps:

1.   Log in to Google+.

2. Start typing the name of the person you're looking for in the Search Google+ search box.

   Google+ returns all results as you're typing, and it starts by returning the people already in your circles who match your query. **Figure 1.33** shows the results for **john**, displaying everyone in my circles whose name or profile page contains the text *john*.

   When you finish typing your search query, the final result appears (**Figure 1.34**).

3. Click the person you want to add to check out his or her full profile page (**Figure 1.35**).

Figure 1.33 People search returns matches from your circles first, followed by matches outside your circles.

Figure 1.34 Google+ people search found one of my favorite authors: John Scalzi.

Figure 1.35 John Scalzi's profile page.

If you want to add this person to some of your circles, click the red Add to Circles button on the profile page. For more information about circles, see Chapter 2.

 tip Google+ search can also be used for other things; check out Chapter 6 for everything you want to know about searching on Google+.

Googling for Google+

You can also use a plain old Google search to find people on Google+. Follow these steps:

1. Go to www.google.com.

2. Enter your search terms.

   For this exercise, search for me—and look for my Google+ profile in particular. To do, append google+ to my name, making your search term *scott mcnulty google+*.

3. Click the Google Search button.

   Figure 1.36 shows that Google found my profile (the first result!), as well as a few other Scott McNultys who are using Google+, though they seem to have neglected filling out their profile information.

Figure 1.36 You can use plain old Google to find public Google+ profiles like mine.

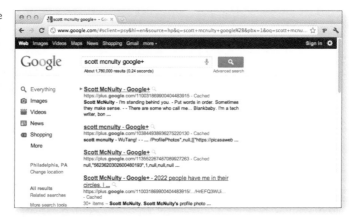

Searching third-party directories

Some intrepid Google+ users think that finding people on the service isn't as easy as it could be, so they've created online directories that attempt to make it easier. Keep in mind that these sites aren't affiliated with Google in any way. They simply gather all the public profile data that people share and present it in a different format.

All these sites function in pretty much the same way, so in this section, I cover the one I like best: Find People on Plus, at www.findpeopleonplus .com (**Figure 1.37**).

Figure 1.37 Find People on Plus is one of many third-party directories that are trying to become the phone book of Google+.

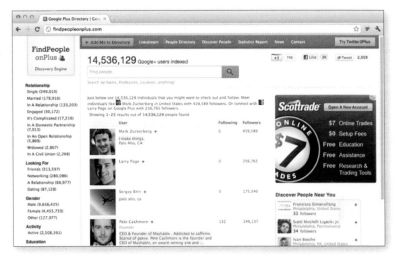

This site gives you a couple of ways to . . . well, find people on Google+. The home page lists people who have lots of followers. The logic for inclusion seems to be that the more people follow a person, the more interesting that person is. (Interestingly, in September 2011, Facebook's founder Mark Zuckerberg had the most followers on Google+, beating out both Google co-founders, who were second and third in the list.)

To get to someone's Google+ profile page, mouse over the little plus sign displayed next to that person's name. The plus sign changes to a little folder (**Figure 1.38**), which you click to go to that person's Google+ profile.

Figure 1.38 Clicking the folder takes you to that person's Google+ profile.

Find People on Plus also allows you to search its directory with keywords; the results look just like the list on the home page.

Finally, Find People on Plus places people in groups. The left column of the home page displays groups based on profile data: Relationship, Looking For, Education, and the like. Clicking any of the items takes you to a list of people within the groups. Then you can add people in those lists to your Google+ circles by visiting their Google+ profiles.

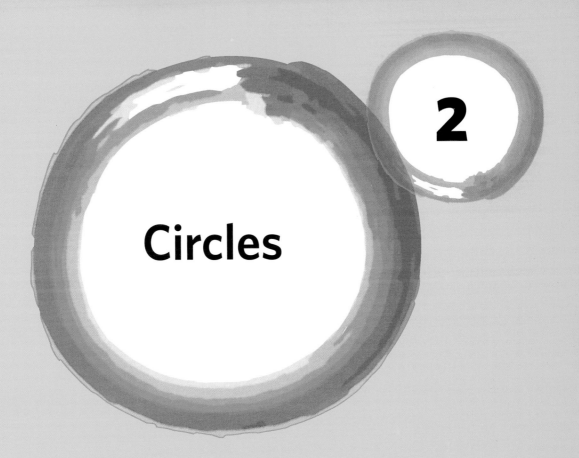

Circles

Circles are so basic to the Google+ experience that I was tempted to start this book by talking about them. Because you can't use circles until you actually have a Google+ account, however, they had to wait until this chapter.

Circles are groups of the people you follow on Google+. One person can be in many circles, and circles can contain many people. (There's a limit of 5,000 people per circle, but I doubt that many circles will hit that limit.)

Still confused? Circles mimic our relationships in the real world to a degree. You deal with different circles of people in day-to-day life: family members, close friends, co-workers, and so on. Because Google+ is about sharing information with people, it makes sense to group those people into similar circles. Then you can choose to share some things (like those pictures you took while out carousing) only with certain people (such as your Drinking Buddies circle).

In this chapter, I cover everything about circles, starting with the default circles and moving on to adding and removing people, creating custom circles, managing existing circles, and sharing your circles.

Working with Circles

Click the Circles icon in the Google+ toolbar (**Figure 2.1**) to manage your circles. In the resulting Circles page (**Figure 2.2**), you can do a variety of things: create new circles, find people, add people to circles, and more. This page is broken into two sections: people in the top section, which I call the *people browser,* and circles in the bottom section, which I call the *circle browser.*

Figure 2.1 The Google+ toolbar.

Circles icon

Figure 2.2 Your circles.

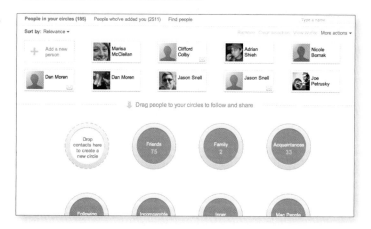

If you're looking at this page for the first time, you'll see only the Google+ default circles listed in the circle browser:

- Friends
- Family
- Acquaintances
- Following

By default, the people browser displays only the people in your circles—as you can tell by looking at the People in Your Circles tab, which is red. That's the active view. The numbers next to this tab are the number of people currently in your circles. Figure 2.2 shows that I have 185 people in various circles of mine.

If you want to see which people have you listed in their own circles, click the People Who've Added You tab, which turns red to show that it's the active tab. Your own circles will still be displayed in the circle browser, but the people browser changes to list everyone who has you in a circle—even people who aren't in any of your circles. Clicking this tab is a great way to make sure that you're following the people of interest who are following you.

Finding people

The people browser can also help you find more people to follow. When you click the Find People tab (**Figure 2.3**), Google+ displays people that it thinks you may want to follow, based on who's already in your circles, who's in your Gmail contacts list (if you use Gmail), and how you're linked to people through any connected accounts in your profile. (Flip back to Chapter 1 for more information about connected accounts.)

Figure 2.3 The Find People tab lists people whom you may be interested in adding to a circle.

The Find People tab gives you three other ways to find people. The Find Friends bar at the top of the page lists three options:

- **Yahoo.** If you have a Yahoo email account, click this link, and log in with your user name and password. Google+ searches your contacts for people.

- **Hotmail.** This link works just like the Yahoo link except that you log in with your Hotmail credentials.

- **Upload Address Book.** What if you have an address book on your computer or on another service that isn't listed? As long as you can export the contents of your address book into a CSV (comma-separated values) file or into vCards, you can use this link to upload those files to Google+. Then you can add those folks to your Google+ circles.

You can set how people show up in the people browser by clicking the Sort By menu in the top-left corner of each tab. **Figure 2.4** on the next page shows the Sort By menu for the People in Your Circles tab, which allows you to sort by Relevance (the default), First Name, Last Name, or Recently Updated. Recently Updated first shows the people who've recently done something on Google+ and then sorts the rest of your people in the order in which they did something on Google+, from most to least recent.

Figure 2.4 People are sorted by relevance by default. You can sort by a few other things.

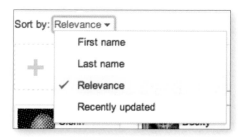

The Sort By menu in the People Who've Added You tab also has a special sort option: Not Yet in Circles. This option is great for finding people who have you in one of their circles but who aren't in a circle of yours.

Adding people to a circle

Now that you know how to find people and see who has you in a circle, it's time to add someone to a circle of your own. Here's what you do:

1. Log in to Google+.

2. Click the Circles icon in the navigation bar to open the Circles page.

3. In the people browser, search for the person you want to add (refer to "Finding people" earlier in this chapter).

    The search in **Figure 2.5** finds people in the People Who've Added You tab sorted by Not Yet in Circles.

Figure 2.5 This tab lists people who have you in their circles but aren't in one of your circles.

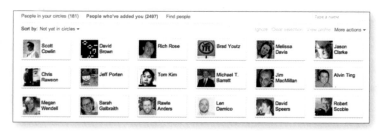

4. Click the person you want to add.

    When you select a person in the people browser, the item turns blue (**Figure 2.6**).

When you hover over a person's picture in the people browser, his name appears along with a snippet from his profile so that you'll know you're adding the right person.

You can select more than one person this way; just click as many people as you want to add to the circle.

5. Drag the selected person into the circle browser, and drop him into the circle you want to add him to (**Figure 2.7**).

A yellow alert at the top of the screen lets you know that the person has been added to your circle, and he receives a notification that you've added him.

When you're dragging multiple people, Google+ displays them as a stack (**Figure 2.8**).

Figure 2.6 (near right) Click a person to select him.

Figure 2.7 (far right) Drag and drop a selected person to add him to a circle.

Figure 2.8 You can select multiple people, and Google+ tells you how many people are in your selection.

 People will be notified when they're added to one of your circles, but they won't be told the name of the circles to which they've been added. You can have a circle named People I Don't Like, for example, and add anyone to it; the people you add will never know.

Removing people from a circle

Just as you can add people to a circle, you can take them out. You have a default circle called Friends, but you know that friendships sometimes end. Here's how to remove someone from a circle:

1. Log in to Google+.

2. Click the Circles icon in the navigation bar to open the Circles page.

3. In the circle browser section, click the circle from which you want to remove the person.

    When you click a circle, the people browser shows only the people that are in that circle (**Figure 2.9**). Also, the selected circle turns gray, with links added, and a new tab appears in red at the top of the people browser: the name of the circle with the number of people in the circle displayed next to it. If you click the X on this tab, the tab closes, and you go back to the People in Your Circles tab.

4. Find the person you're looking to delete.

    You can scroll through the list of people in the selected circle, which can take a while if the circle is crowded, or you can search for the person (refer to "Finding people" earlier in this chapter).

    In the top-right corner of the people browser is a search box containing the text *Type a name* in gray (refer to Figure 2-3). When you type a name in that box, only the people whose names match the query are displayed (**Figure 2.10**).

5. Click the person you want to remove.

Figure 2.9 Display who's in a circle by clicking it.

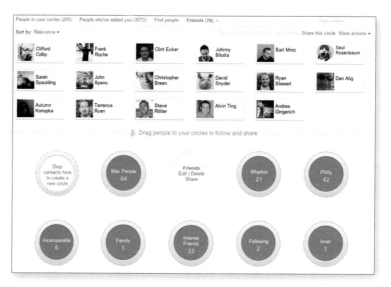

Figure 2.10 Looking for someone in a circle? Just use the filter to show only the people who match your query.

If you want to remove more than one person, that's OK; just click as many people as you want to remove.

When you select a person, a new Selected tab and some action items appear (**Figure 2.11**).

6. Click the Remove action item.

The selected person is removed from your Friends circle—an action that's confirmed by a yellow message at the top of the page.

Figure 2.11 Select someone to activate some action links, such as Remove.

 If you decide that you were a little hasty in your removal, click the Undo link in the confirmation message, and the person you deleted is added back.

Creating a custom circle

When you start following a bunch of people on Google+, you'll find that the default circles just don't cut it for all the groups of people that you know. That's why you can create as many circles as you want and name them whatever you like. A circle can have a single member (I have a circle called Inner that has only my wife in it, should I want to share something only with her), or it can have as many as 5,000 people (in case you have an incredible number of siblings, perhaps).

I recommend creating two general groups of circles:

- **Relationship-based.** We all have different types of relationships: friends, co-workers, Internet friends, and more (even friends who are also co-workers!). Create circles to reflect these relationships, and organize people in those circles. My co-worker friends, for example, end up in both my Friends circle and my Wharton circle because I work at Wharton Computing.

- **Interest-based.** Google+ has lots of interesting people who are sharing interesting things, but they aren't necessarily people you know. They don't belong in relationship-based circles, but you still want to group them somehow. You could create a couple of circles devoted to a particular topic (I have a Google+ circle for Google people who work on Google+, for example) or geography (for people who live in a particular area).

Suppose that you follow a lot of people who have the same first name: Dan. Why not create a circle called The Dans and put everyone who's named Dan in it? Just follow these steps:

1. Log in to Google+.

2. Click the Circles icon in the navigation bar to open the Circles page.

3. Make sure that you're on the People in Your Circles tab so that the name search will find all the people you follow.

4. Type **Dan** in the name filter box, and select all the resulting Dans (**Figure 2.12**).

Figure 2.12 All the Dans I know—on Google+, anyway.

 The search results return people who are already in your circles first, followed by people you don't follow but may be interested in following. Feel free to drag any of those interesting people into your circles.

5. Drag the people you've selected to the circle browser, and drop them on the icon titled Drop Contacts Here to Create a New Circle (**Figure 2.13**).

6. To create the circle you just populated, click the Create Circle link (**Figure 2.14**), or click Clear if you've changed your mind.

    When you click Create Circle, the circle editor opens.

Figure 2.13 (near right) Create a new circle by dropping people on this icon.

Figure 2.14 (far right) Click Create Circle to do just that.

7. Give your circle a name and a description (maximum 500 characters), if you like (**Figure 2.15**).

8. If you forgot to add someone who should be in this circle, click the Add a New Person icon, and follow the onscreen directions.

9. When you're done, click the blue Create Circle with x People button.

   Google+ creates your new circle (**Figure 2.16**). Now you can share items with just those folks and check out what they've been posting to Google+. (For more on both of those topics, see Chapter 3.)

Figure 2.15 Every circle needs a name; descriptions are optional.

Figure 2.16 The Dans circle has been created.

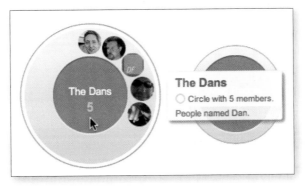

Managing Your Circles

So far in this chapter, you've spent a lot of time interacting with the people browser, but you can do a lot with the circle browser, such as rearrange, rename, reorganize, and delete existing circles. I cover all these topics in this section.

Moving circles

The order in which your circles appear in the circle browser may not matter to you, but it affects how you use Google+. When you're looking at your stream, five of your circles are displayed, with the rest hidden in the More section (**Figure 2.17**). The order of your circles in the circle browser determines the order of the list of your circles in your stream.

To rearrange your circles, just drag the circle you want to move to its new position (**Figure 2.18**). Your stream circle list updates automatically to reflect this new order (**Figure 2.19**).

Figure 2.17 Your circles are displayed next to your stream.

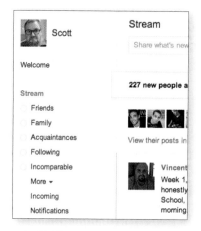

Figure 2.18 (near right) Reorder your circles in the circle browser to change their order in your stream.

Figure 2.19 (far right) Reordered circles.

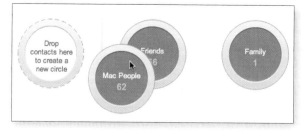

Editing names and descriptions

When you create a circle, you have the chance to name it and add a description (refer to "Creating a custom circle" earlier in this chapter).

These items aren't set in stone, however; you can change them however you like. To do that, follow these steps:

1. Log in to Google+.

2. Click the Circles icon in the navigation bar to open the Circles page.

3. Click the circle that you want to rename.

   The circle turns gray, and Edit, Delete, and Share links appear (**Figure 2.20**).

4. Click the Edit link.

   A mini circle editor opens (**Figure 2.21**).

5. Type a new name and description in the appropriate text boxes, and click Save.

   Now the circle formerly known as Acquaintances is called Internet Friends and has a new description (**Figure 2.22**).

Figure 2.20 (near right)
The Edit link allows you to change the name and/or description of the selected circle.

Figure 2.21 (far right)
Editable circle details.

Figure 2.22 My newly renamed circle. I love my Internet friends.

 You can also edit a circle by right-clicking it and choosing Edit Circle from the shortcut menu.

Removing or moving people

You know how to remove people from circles by using the people browser (refer to "Removing people from a circle" earlier in this chapter). To a lesser degree, you can do the same thing in the circle browser. When you hover your mouse over a circle, it expands and displays up to 13 people who are in that circle. If the circle has more than 13 members, the 13 most relevant people (as determined by Google+) are displayed (**Figure 2.23**).

When you hover over a person in the circle, his or her name appears (**Figure 2.24**).

Figure 2.23 (near right) Hovering over a circle displays up to 13 circle members.

Figure 2.24 (far right) You can delete or move this circle member.

Click that person to do one of two things:

- **Drag him out of the circle.** Just drag the person to an area of the circle browser outside all your circles. A red trash-can icon appears as you drag (**Figure 2.25**). When you release the mouse button, the person you dragged is deleted from the circle.

 This action removes the person from this circle only. If he's listed in more than one of your circles, his other memberships aren't affected. If this circle is the only one of yours he was in, however, dragging him out removes him from your stream.

- **Drag him to another circle.** Just click a person in your circle and drag him over the circle you want to add him to. A little green icon appears as you drag (**Figure 2.26**). When you release the mouse button, the person you dragged is added to the new circle and is still in the original circle too.

Figure 2.25 (near right)
Drag a member out of a circle to remove him.

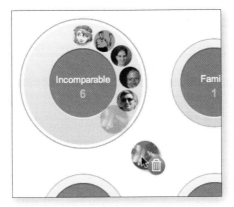

Figure 2.26 (far right)
Drop a circle member to another circle to add him to that circle.

Deleting circles

Deleting a circle (including the default circles) that you no longer use is easy, but you need to know a few things before you do:

- When you delete a circle, anyone who is in that circle only is removed from your list of contacts in Google+. People who are in multiple circles aren't deleted, and their other circle memberships aren't affected.

- Stuff that you've shared with the members of this circle will no longer be viewable by them unless they're also members of another circle that can see the shared items.

With those caveats out of the way, you're ready to delete some circles. Follow these steps:

1. Click the circle that you want to delete.

    Edit, Delete, and Share links appear (refer to Figure 2.20).

2. Click the Delete link.

    A confirmation dialog box appears, displaying some warnings (**Figure 2.27** on the next page).

3. Click the blue Delete Circle button.

    The circle rolls off the screen into oblivion.

 You can also delete a circle by right-clicking it and choosing Delete Circle from the shortcut menu.

Figure 2.27 Deleting a circle has consequences.

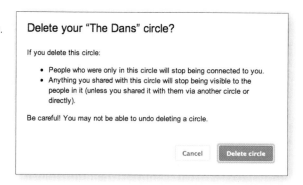

Delete your "The Dans" circle?

If you delete this circle:

- People who were only in this circle will stop being connected to you.
- Anything you shared with this circle will stop being visible to the people in it (unless you shared it with them via another circle or directly).

Be careful! You may not be able to undo deleting a circle.

Cancel   **Delete circle**

If you deleted a circle in haste, you can sometimes restore the circle by clicking the Undo link in the yellow confirmation message (**Figure 2.28**). This method doesn't work all the time, so be sure you're certain that you want to delete a circle—and that you've selected the correct circle—before you delete.

Figure 2.28 The circle is gone, but you may be able to restore it by clicking Undo.

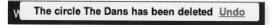

The circle The Dans has been deleted Undo

What Circles Are Your People In?

You've added people to all sorts of circles now, and you're curious to see exactly what circles people are in before you share something that you don't want everyone to see. (Hey, that's what circles are for!) Whenever you hover over someone's profile while you're logged in to Google+, a pop-up window lists the circles you've included that person in. This technique works on your stream, on the person's profile page, and in the people browser.

When you hover over a person in the people browser, that person's circles are also highlighted in the circle browser (**Figure 2.29**). If you don't want to share something with that person, you can share it in a circle that isn't highlighted.

Figure 2.29 Hover over a person to see what circles he or she is in.

Getting Change Notifications

Whenever you add someone to one of your circles, he or she gets a notification of this fact. You're also notified when someone adds you to a circle. You won't know the name of the circle to which you've been added (feel free to create a Handsome Authors circle and add me to it), but you'll know that someone is interested in what you have to say on Google+.

By default, your notification is an email alert (**Figure 2.30**). The email includes the name of the person who added you and his or her profile picture. Clicking the picture takes you to that person's profile page, where you can add him or her to any of your circles by clicking the red Add to Circles button in the top-right corner (**Figure 2.31**). A menu appears, listing all your circles in the order in which you arranged them in the circle browser (**Figure 2.32**). Click each circle you want to add the person to. You can even create a circle by clicking the Create New Circle link.

Figure 2.30 (near right) When you're added to someone's circle, you're notified via email.

Figure 2.31 (far right) If someone has you in a circle, his profile says so.

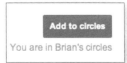

In addition to sending email notifications, Google+ uses the Plus bar to display a variety of notifications, such as telling you when someone has added you to a circle. The number of notifications is displayed in red (**Figure 2.33**). This display goes up to 9; if you get more than 9 notifications, the display reads 9+.

Click the number in the Plus bar to reveal the Notifications menu, which lists all your notifications, new and old (**Figure 2.34**). As soon as you open the Notifications menu, the counter resets to 0.

Figure 2.32 (near right)
Clicking the Add to
Circles button brings up
your list of circles and
the option to create a
new one on the spot.

Figure 2.33 (far right)
Notifications are also displayed in the Plus bar.

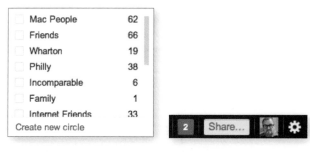

Figure 2.34 Notifications
are grouped by type.

Now you can take some actions on the various notifications, which are
grouped by types denoted by the icon to the right. A green circle signifies
notifications that concern circles. (The top notification in Figure 2.34, for
example, says that 10 people have added me to their Google+ circles.)
Click a notification to see each of the individual notifications. As you can
see in **Figure 2.35**, each notification includes an Add to Circles button.
Hover over that button to bring up your list of circles; then click the circle
you want to add the person to or create a new one.

You can also ignore the person or all the people who added you in a batch.
The concept of ignoring someone is covered in Chapter 3.

Figure 2.35 You can
add people to circles
right from the
Notifications menu.

Sharing Your Circles

Your circles are very personal things, and as I mention earlier in this chapter, the people listed in your circles have no way of knowing which circles they're in. Depending on how you use circles, you may want to share some of them with other people on Google+.

Perhaps you're a panelist in a podcast, and you've made a circle composed of your fellow panelists. Here's how to share that circle with your stream:

1. Click the Circles icon in the Google+ toolbar to open the Circles page.
2. Click the circle you want to share.

    Edit, Delete, and Share links appear (refer to Figure 2.20).
3. Click Share.

    The Share Circle box appears, with your circle smack dab in the middle.
4. Add a comment, and specify the people with whom you want to share this circle (**Figure 2.36**).

 **Keep in mind that the people with whom you share a circle will be able to see all the members of the circle and add them to circles of their own.**

5. Click the green Share button.

    The circle is posted to your stream (**Figure 2.37** on the next page). Now when people see that circle in their stream, they can click the blue View People in Circle button to see who's in the circle.

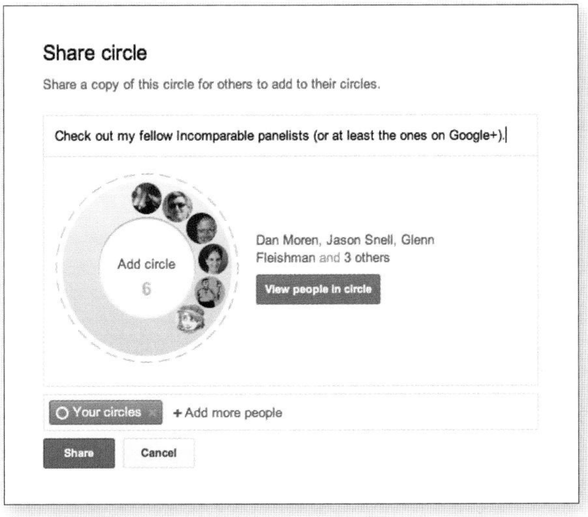

Figure 2.36 Sharing a circle with your stream.

Share circle

Share a copy of this circle for others to add to their circles.

Check out my fellow incomparable panelists (or at least the ones on Google+).

Add circle

6

Dan Moren, Jason Snell, Glenn Fleishman and 3 others

View people in circle

○ Your circles   + Add more people

Share   Cancel

Figure 2.37 A shared circle posted to the stream.

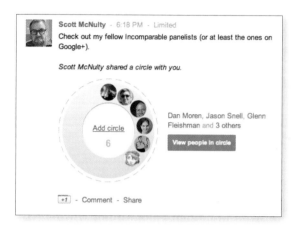

If you can see a shared circle, you can also add its members to an existing circle of your own or create a new one, as follows:

1. Click the View People in Circle button to see the members of the shared circle.

2. Click the people you want to add to the circle.

3. Type the name of the existing or new circle to which you want to add those people (**Figure 2.38**).

4. Click the Create or Add to Circles button.

Figure 2.38 You can add people from a shared circle to a new, or existing, circle.

Dipping into the Stream

3

If Google+ were a three-legged stool, which it isn't, the first two legs would be your Google+ account and circles. The final leg of this hypothetical stool would be the stream. Everything people in your circles share with you is displayed in your stream.

This chapter covers how to post to your stream, how to make sure you're sharing with only the people you want to share with, and how to manage your stream so that you're not seeing stuff you have no interest in. It also covers what you can do with other people's posts, including commenting on them and sharing them.

Sharing Overview

The first thing you'll want to do is post something to your stream (**Figure 3.1**). Posting content to your stream is known as *sharing* in Google+ vernacular. At the top of your stream is the sharing box, ready for you to start typing in.

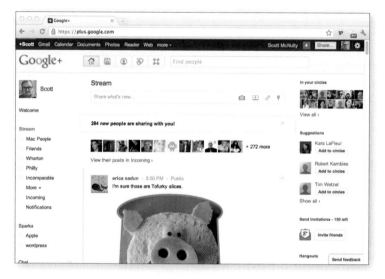

In addition to text, you can share the following types of things:

- Pictures
- Videos
- Links
- Your location

Location is a little special because it can be appended to any of the other post types. (Obviously, the text post type is just text, but you can also include location data.) You can't post a picture and a video in the same post, however.

The following sections take a look at how you put together something to share on your stream. Each post in a stream has three components: the text box, the post type, and the people/circles you're sharing with.

Text box

The most basic part of any post in Google+ is text. In **Figure 3.2**, I've entered some text in the sharing box and formatted it using the limited options available today on Google+:

- For **boldface,** type *Bold*.
- For *italics,* type _Italics_.
- For ~~strikethrough~~, type -Strikeouts-.

Figure 3.2 Formatting options in the text field of the sharing box are limited but useful.

Let's say you follow someone on Google+, and you want to make sure that person notices something you're sharing. Type either a plus sign (+) or at symbol (@) and the first few letters of the person's name in the text box to mention her in your post. As you type, Google+ lists people in your circle who match what you're typing (**Figure 3.3**). Click the person you want to mention, and a link to her profile is inserted (**Figure 3.4**). This little trick also automatically shares the post with the person you mentioned.

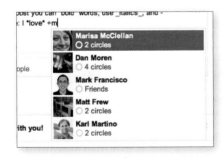

Figure 3.3 (left) Mention another Google+ user by typing + or @ and the name in the sharing box and selecting that person from your circles.

Figure 3.4 (above) Mentioning someone automatically adds her to the people with whom this post is shared.

When you're ready to share your post, just click the Share button (**Figure 3.5**).

Figure 3.5 A post in the stream that uses formatting and mentions someone.

 You can mention as many people as you like in a post.

Some things to keep in mind when mentioning people in posts: A mentioned person might receive a notification that he or she has been mentioned in the post. No matter who you share the post with, even if it's just with one person, anyone mentioned in a post will be able to see the post.

Post types

At the bottom right of the sharing box are four little icons that represent the available post types (**Figure 3.6**). From left to right, the icons allow you to share a photo (or photos), video, a link, or your location. I'll take a look at the types in order so you can see the differences.

Photos

If you have any type of image you want to post to your stream (including, but not limited to, funny pictures of kitties, family photos, and animated GIFs), all you have to do is click the little green camera to bring up the photo sharing options (**Figure 3.7**).

Figure 3.6 (near right) The icons for the various things you can share on Google+: photos, video, links, and your location.

Figure 3.7 (far right) The photo sharing options.

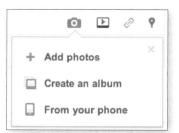

Add Photos. The first option is the most straightforward. Click Add Photos, and a file browser appears. Select the picture you want to upload to Google+ from your computer, and click Open or OK. The image is uploaded and attached to your post, without text for the moment (**Figure 3.8**).

Figure 3.8 Add Photos allows you to upload pictures directly to your post.

Right under the photo are two options: Edit Photos and Add More. Clicking Add More brings up the file browser again so you can select and upload another picture. (Keep clicking Add More to add more and more pictures to this post.)

Edit Photos brings up the photo editor (**Figure 3.9**). Hovering your mouse over a photo makes three icons appear at the bottom of the photo: Rotate Counterclockwise, Rotate Clockwise, and Delete. Click the Add Caption link to add a caption to your photo (**Figure 3.10**). Press Return or Enter to save the caption or Esc to clear whatever you've entered.

Figure 3.9 (near right) Google+ has some rudimentary photo-editing options, including rotation.

Figure 3.10 (far right) Adding a caption gives people a little more information about the photo.

Create an Album. While you can upload multiple images using the Add Photos option, that can get pretty tedious. If you want to share multiple photos, use the Create an Album option.

Clicking this link brings up the album creator (**Figure 3.11**). You can add photos to an album by clicking the blue Select Photos from Your Computer button or by selecting some pictures from your computer and dragging them into the dotted-line box.

Figure 3.11 Creating an album is a great way to upload more than one related photo at a time.

Either way, the photos start to upload into this new album (**Figure 3.12**). By default, Google+ uses the current date as the name of your album, which probably isn't what you want to call it. Enter a name of your own in the Album Name field.

Figure 3.12 I'm uploading three photos into my Gettysburg album.

Hover over a picture in the album creator to add a caption or use one of the three available actions (two rotates and delete).

When you're happy with your album, click the blue Create Album button, and the album is ready to share (**Figure 3.13**). One main image is shown, with the rest of the images in the album displayed along the bottom of the post.

Figure 3.13 The album in the sharing box.

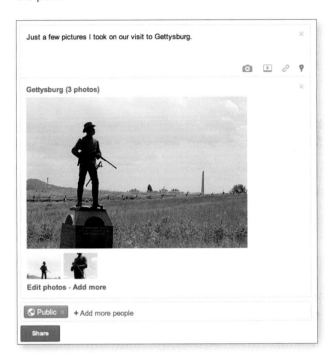

From Your Phone. This interesting option works only if you have the Google+ Android app installed on your phone. If you don't have the app installed or aren't using an Android device, clicking this option just shows you a message prompting you to install the app (**Figure 3.14**). This option is covered in Chapter 5.

Figure 3.14 The Android app is required to use the From Your Phone option.

When your photos are posted, they show up in the streams of everyone with whom they were shared (**Figure 3.15** on the next page). People can comment on them, share them, or even tag people in the photos. (The tagging functionality is covered in Chapter 5 as well.)

Videos

Click the green video button in the share box to insert/upload a video to your stream. As with sharing pictures, you have three methods of choosing a video (or videos) to share (**Figure 3.16**).

Figure 3.15 (near right)
A photo album (top) and a single photo (bottom) are shared in my stream.

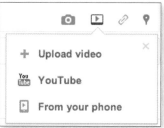

Figure 3.16 (far right)
The video sharing options.

Upload Video. If you have a video on your computer that you want to share, this is the option for you. Click the Upload Video link, and the video uploader appears (**Figure 3.17**). It looks and functions much like the photo uploader. Either click the blue Select Videos from Your Computer button to browse your computer's file system or just drag the movies you want to upload into the dotted-line box. Google+ displays the file name of the video and the upload progress (**Figure 3.18**).

 The time required to upload a video depends greatly on two things: file size and upload speeds. The smaller the file, the less time uploading takes. At fast upload speeds, even large files upload quickly.

Figure 3.17 (above)
Drag a video into the dotted-line box to start the upload.

Figure 3.18 (above right)
The video-upload progress is shown here.

Google+ has to process the video for playback. Processing time varies depending on how large the video file is. The blue Add Videos button is disabled until all the videos you've uploaded have finished processing.

When processing completes, a thumbnail of your video appears, with a Play button on it (**Figure 3.19**). Clicking the Play button plays your video in the uploader. This is a great way to make sure that nothing has gone awry with the processing.

Figure 3.19　One video has been uploaded.

If you want to add a few more videos, click the Upload More link to add them. When your videos are all set, click the blue Add Videos button to share them.

The videos you uploaded appear under the text area of the share box. Unlike with photos, you can't add a caption or any other type of descriptive text to the video itself, so make sure to include some explanation in the text of the post.

Click Share when you're happy with your videos and they're posted to your stream.

YouTube. If you're just looking to share a cute kitty video or the latest viral video with your friends, the YouTube link of the video sharing menu is for you (refer to Figure 3.16).

When you click the YouTube link, you're taken to the YouTube sharing interface, with three options listed on the left side (**Figure 3.20**). By default, the search option is selected. Enter a search term for the video you want to share. In Figure 3.20, I've searched for Japan's most famous feline: Maru.

Figure 3.20 Searching YouTube for the perfect Maru video to share.

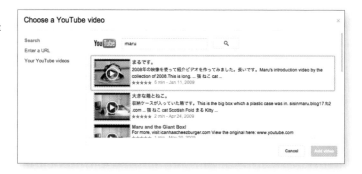

The results show a thumbnail of the video, the title (in Japanese in Figure 3.20), a bit of the YouTube description, as well as the video's rating and when it was posted. The currently selected video is outlined in blue.

Click the video's thumbnail to enlarge the preview and watch the video right in the YouTube search-results interface (**Figure 3.21**). When you've found the video you're looking for, click the Add Video button, and the selected video will be ready to share with your stream (**Figure 3.22**).

Figure 3.21 Click a search result to preview it.

Figure 3.22 A YouTube
video in the sharing box.

Figure 3.22 A YouTube
video in the sharing box.

 Don't want to share the video you selected after all? Click the X in the top-right
corner of the video section.

If you have the URL of a YouTube video (perhaps someone posted it to
Twitter or just emailed you the link directly), click the Enter a URL link on
the left side and paste it in the text field (**Figure 3.23** on the next page).
As soon as the link is pasted, the YouTube video appears, so you can
watch it and make sure that you have the correct video of a kitten being
surprised. (Yep, that's the one.)

Click Add Video, and the video is ready to share.

The last option in the YouTube sharing screen is useful only if you have a
YouTube channel of your own. If you do have a YouTube channel, clicking
Your YouTube Videos displays a list of your YouTube videos (**Figure 3.24**
on the next page). This list functions just like the YouTube search-results
list in the search screen. Click the video you want to share to highlight it
in blue and play a preview of the video. Click Add Video to share it.

Figure 3.23 Paste the URL of a YouTube video here to share it. The video is previewed.

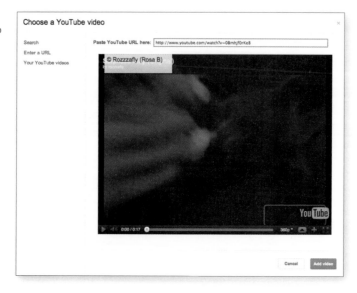

From Your Phone. The final way to share video is From Your Phone. This option requires that you have an Android device running the Google+ app (see Chapter 7). The app can automatically upload any video you take on your phone to a private album on Google+. When you click the From Your Phone link, all the movies uploaded from your phone are listed (**Figure 3.25**). Clicking any of the videos listed selects it and allows you to preview it. Click the Add Videos button to insert the video.

Figure 3.24 (below left) If you have a YouTube account with videos, those videos are listed in the Your YouTube Videos tab.

Figure 3.25 (above right)   Videos from an Android phone with the Google+ app installed.

No matter which method you follow to share video, the post to your stream looks pretty similar. **Figure 3.26** shows a YouTube video that I shared with my stream.

Figure 3.26 A shared YouTube video in the stream.

When you share a video you've uploaded directly to Google+, display of the video and playback work a little differently. Clicking the video opens the video's player page, where the video is displayed, and any comments on the post are listed to the video's right (**Figure 3.27**).

Figure 3.27 Clicking a video uploaded to Google+ opens that video's page and displays any comments on the post.

Links

Click the Link icon in the share box to bring up the link box (**Figure 3.28** on the next page). Paste or type a link in the box and then click the Add button. Google+ looks at the link and fetches the page's title, a description, and an image from the page to use as a thumbnail (**Figure 3.29** on the next page).

Figure 3.28 Paste a link to share it.

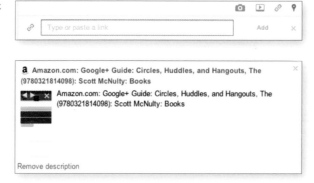

Figure 3.29 Google+ inserts a description and a thumbnail automatically.

If the image Google+ chooses isn't very good, click the arrows at the top of the image to cycle through other possibilities from the page. Stop when you find one you're happy with (**Figure 3.30**). If you don't like any of the options, click the X to clear the image, and no thumbnail will appear next to your link.

Figure 3.30 You can set the thumbnail yourself by clicking the white arrows and cycling through images on the page.

The description is generated from the page you're linking. If you aren't a fan of the description, you can delete it by clicking the Remove Description link. The thumbnail and link both remain, sans description.

Click Share, and your link is posted to your stream (**Figure 3.31**). As with any link, the people you shared this with can click it to visit the page. Make sure you pick a good thumbnail to encourage clicking.

 The appearance of the Share link depends on what you're linking to. Most links will be displayed like the Amazon link in Figure 3.31, but if you paste a link to YouTube, the video will be embedded instead of a thumbnail. (This also works for Vimeo.com links.)

Figure 3.31 A shared link posted to my stream. (That looks like a good book!)

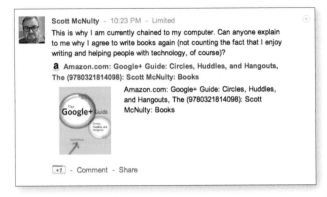

Location

Figure 3.32 The red pin is the Location icon.

Add your current location to anything you post on Google+ by clicking the Location icon in the share box (**Figure 3.32**). Location data can be added to any post type.

Because you're viewing Google+ in a browser, your browser must support geolocation. If it doesn't, the location feature won't work.

Depending on your browser settings, you may see a warning when you click the Location icon, like one shown in **Figure 3.33**. This warning is meant to prevent Web sites from determining your physical location without your knowledge. Because you initiated the location check, allow Google+ to get your location.

Figure 3.33 Google+ asks your browser for location data. Most browsers will ask you to allow this information to be reported.

Google+ figures out your location based on information from your Internet service provider and displays it (**Figure 3.34**). If you hover your mouse over the location, you'll notice that it isn't just text, but a link. Click the link to see the location Google+ displayed on Google Maps.

Figure 3.34 Location can be added to any post type.

If you decide against including your location information with a post (perhaps the location is a little too accurate, and you aren't comfortable sharing it), just click the X in the location box to remove it.

When you're happy with the location data appended to your post, click Share, and the item (with location) is shared on your stream (**Figure 3.35**).

Figure 3.35 A picture of me shared on my stream with my location.

 The location in the stream is also a link to a Google Map.

Setting Who You're Sharing With

In Chapter 2, I show you how to set up circles: groups of people on Google+ that you follow. Each circle has related people in it: friends, family members, and so on. You can share items just with particular circles or even with particular people (or one person).

Above the green Share button is the circle box. In **Figure 3.36**, the post is set to be shared with the public. This means that anyone, logged into Google+ or not, will be able to see whatever I'm sharing. This post will also show up in search-engine results.

If you'd rather limit who can view this item, just click the X in the green Public icon to remove it and then do the following:

1.   Click the Add Circles or People to Share With link (**Figure 3.37**).

The circle/people selector appears (**Figure 3.38**). All the circles you created are listed here (click the More link to see all your circles listed), as well as three special groups:

- **Your Circles.** Anyone in any of your circles will be able to see a post shared with this group.

- **Extended Circles.** Anyone in your circles, and anyone in their circles, will be able to see items shared with this group. Think of this as two degrees of Google+ separation.

- **Public.** You're sharing this item with the world.

Figure 3.36 (below)
The Public icon means anyone will be able to see this post.

Figure 3.37 (above)
Click the link to add circles/people to share this post with.

Figure 3.38 (above right)
Your circles are listed, as are the three built-in groups.

2. Select a circle that you want to share by clicking it in the list or typing its name in the text box.

   You can share the same item with multiple circles. Each circle appears as a blue icon with a circle and its name displayed on it (**Figure 3.39**).

3. If you want to share an item with a particular person, just type his or her name.

   Google+ generates a list of possible matches based on what you've typed, with people from your circles listed first (**Figure 3.40**).

4. Click the name to add that person to the sharing box (**Figure 3.41**).

Figure 3.39 The blue icons represent circles that this post will be visible to.

Figure 3.40 (near right)
Sharing with a particular person is as easy as typing a name.

Figure 3.41 (far right)
This post will be shared with Marisa, and only Marisa.

5. Add people to the sharing box by clicking the Add More People link.

6. Repeat steps 2–5 until you've added all the people/circles you want to share this item with.

    Here's an example. I've decided that I want to share this item with my lovely wife, Marisa, and with my podcasting buddies in a circle called Incomparable. I create my post, add Marisa and the Incomparable circle, and make sure to remove the Public circle (**Figure 3.42**).

    Just before I click the Share button, I want to make sure that I remember who is in the Incomparable circle. I hover over the blue circle icon, and the first three people in the circle are listed, as well as the total number of people in this circle (**Figure 3.43**).

 You can check the Notify About This Post box to alert to everyone in the circle about the item you've shared with them. By default, this box is unchecked because the item will show up in circle members' streams anyway (if they're following you, of course).

Figure 3.42 (above left)
Who will be able to see this post? Marisa and anyone in the Incomparable circle.

Figure 3.43 (above right)
Click a circle's icon to see the first three people in the circle.

Because there are six people in this circle, I want to see all of them, so I click the View All link, and a circle editor appears (**Figure 3.44**).

I can edit the circle as I see fit here. (See Chapter 2 for more information.)

Figure 3.44 The View All link displays everyone in the circle.

7. Click Save if you've made any changes.

   You return to the sharing box.

8. Click the Share button when you're all set with your circles/people and the item is posted to your stream.

   You can tell when a post has been shared with a certain set of people because it's labeled Limited right next to the time the post was posted. If you click Limited, you're able to see with whom the post was shared (**Figure 3.45**). Post shared with the public group are marked Public, and those shared with your extended circles are marked Extended Circles.

Figure 3.45 Posts shared with certain people/circles are denoted as Limited.

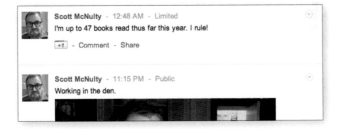

Interacting with Posts

When a post hits the stream, the fun isn't over. In this section, I show you how to edit a post, share someone else's post, link to a post, comment, use Google+'s Plus bar and +1 button, and mute people's posts. (You'll thank me about the last one especially.)

Commenting on posts

By default, you can comment on any Google+ posts in your stream. If you're the first person to leave a comment, you'll see a Comment link at the bottom of the post. Click that link, and the comment entry field appears (**Figure 3.46**). Type your comment, and click Post Comment (**Figure 3.47**). Keep in mind that anyone who can see the post will also be able to see your comment.

Figure 3.46 (above)
Write a comment and click the Post Comment button.

Figure 3.47 (right)   My very helpful comment is displayed for all to see.

 You can mention people, and format text, in comments just like you can in the sharing box. See the "Text box" section earlier in this chapter for details.

When a post already has comments, a comment field is available. Just start typing your comment (**Figure 3.48**).

After you've left a comment, you can always edit it by clicking the Edit link (**Figure 3.49**). You can change the text of your comment or delete it if you've thought better of leaving a comment.

Figure 3.48 (below)
The comment field on posts with comments.

Add a comment...

Figure 3.49 (right)
Click the Edit link to change your comment.

Sharing posts

Your own posts make up a small part of the stream; the rest come from the people in your circles. Suppose that a friend of yours posts something that you think people in your circles would be interested in. You can actually repost, or share, your friend's post.

 Remember that people on Google+ can share things with limited groups of people. If the post you want to share is marked Limited, consider with whom you're planning to share it.

Sharing someone else's post is pretty easy. Follow these steps:

1. Find the post you want to share.

2. Click the Share link at the bottom of the post.

   The Share This Post interface appears (**Figure 3.50**).

Figure 3.50 Share other people's Google+ posts from this form.

3. Add some commentary in the text box.

4. Set which circles/people you want to share the post with.

5. Click Share.

   This post is shared with your selected circles (**Figure 3.51** on the next page).

When someone shares one of your posts, you'll get notified. All the people who share a post in this manner are listed below the original post (**Figure 3.52** on the next page).

Figure 3.51 Brett's post shared by me on my stream.

Figure 3.52 Each post lists how many times it has been shared and by whom.

 Disabling sharing for posts is covered in the "Taking other post actions" section later in this chapter.

Using the Plus bar and +1 button

There are a couple of other ways you can post items to your stream: using the Plus bar or the +1 button on participating Web sites.

Plus bar

One of the interesting things about the black Plus bar (see Chapter 1 for more information) is the sharing box incorporated into it. Click the box labeled Share, and the full share box is revealed (**Figure 3.53**). All the features of the sharing box are available on the Plus bar; you can share text, pictures, videos, and your location with only the circles you choose.

 At the moment, the Plus bar doesn't appear on too many Google sites other than Google+ itself and Google.com.

+1 button

You've probably noticed that every post on Google+ sports a +1 button. So do any comments left on posts.

Figure 3.53 You can share right from the Plus bar.

To +1 a post (meaning that you enjoyed that post or support it), just click its +1 button (**Figure 3.54**). The number of +1s a post has received is listed below the post. If you click that number, the people who +1ed it are displayed (**Figure 3.55**).

Figure 3.54 (above)
+1ing a post is also shown below the post.

Figure 3.55 (right)
Hover over the number of +1s to see who the +1s are from.

To +1 a comment, just hover your mouse over the comment, and click the +1 button that appears (**Figure 3.56** on the next page). The number of +1s is displayed next to the comment, which makes using comments for polls possible. In Figure 3.56, I posted a question with two choices to my stream. I left two comments that each offered one of the choices. People voted for their choice by +1ing the appropriate comment, making a crude poll.

Taking other post actions

In addition to commenting, sharing, and +1ing posts, you can take a few more actions on posts. The available actions differ, depending on whether the post is one you wrote or someone else's post. Either way, clicking the little triangle in the top-right corner lists the actions (**Figure 3.57** on the next page).

Actions for your posts

Figure 3.57 shows the actions that are available for a post you wrote:

Figure 3.57 (above right)
The actions available to you on your own posts.

- **Edit This Post.** You can change any of the text you entered, and remove a photo, video, link, or location from a post, by using the Edit This Post action (**Figure 3.58**).

  When you're happy with your edits, click the blue Save button. Edited posts are denoted with the word *Edited* in parentheses next to the updated time stamp (**Figure 3.59**).

Figure 3.58 Editing a post.

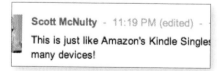

- **Delete This Post.** Post something that no amount of editing can fix? Share something with the wrong circle? Click Delete This Post, and a warning appears, asking if you're sure (**Figure 3.60**). Click the blue Delete button, and the post is gone. There's no undo.

- **Link to This Post.** Every post on Google+ has a permalink that points directly to it. This allows you to send a link to a post to your friends who may not be on Google+. The Link to This Post action opens the post's permalink in your browser so you can copy it (**Figure 3.61**).

 This action appears only for public posts.

- **Report or Remove Comments.** This action is available only for your posts that have comments. Clicking this action makes a couple of icons appear next to each comment on the post (**Figure 3.62** on the next page). The top icon (the X) deletes the comment. The bottom icon (the flag) flags the comment for inappropriate language.

Figure 3.60 Deleting a post removes it from Google+.

Figure 3.61 Public posts have permalinks you can share with anyone.

- **Disable Comments.** You can disable comments on posts with or without comments. Clicking this action simply removes the Comment link and box, so no one can leave a comment (or additional comments if some have already been left). This action turns into Enable Comments when clicked, allowing you to turn comments back on.

- **Lock This Post.** Google+ is all about sharing, but what if you post something to a limited group of people and want to be sure they don't share it? Lock This Post removes the share option, and the word *Locked* is displayed on the post (**Figure 3.63**).

Figure 3.62 Delete or flag a comment or part of a post.

Scott McNulty - Yesterday 5:29 PM - Mobile - Public (locked)
Current reading material.

Figure 3.63 Locking a post disables sharing, even on a public post.

On locked posts, this action is Unlock This Post.

Actions for other people's posts

The options available to you in the actions menu for other people's posts are slightly different from those that are available for your own:

- **Link to This Post.** Just like the action available for your public posts, this action opens the post's permalink for linking elsewhere (public posts only).

- **Report Abuse.** Click the Report Abuse action, and flag icons appear next to all the parts of the post (including comments, if there are any). Click the icon on the inappropriate part of the post, and select the reason why you're reporting it (**Figure 3.64**). Click Submit, and the flag icon turns red.

  If you want to cancel your report, click the flag icon again.

- **Mute This Post.** What if you don't care about a particular post, but you want to see the person's other posts? Click Mute This Post, and the post—and only that post—is removed from your stream (**Figure 3.65**). Immediately after you mute a post, you have a chance to unmute it by clicking the Undo Mute link.

- **Block This Person.** Sometimes, there are people you want nothing to do with. Click the Block This Person link to block the author of the post (**Figure 3.66**).

Report this post

Thank you for helping Google by reporting content which may be in violation of our Community Standards.

Why are you reporting this post?

◉ Spam
○ Nudity
○ Hate speech or violence
○ Child abuse
○ Copyright
○ Other

Cancel   Submit

No longer seeing this post. Undo mute.

Figure 3.64 (left) When flagging a post, you need to supply a reason.

Figure 3.65 (above) Muting a post hides it from your stream, but you see other posts by the same person.

Figure 3.66 Blocking a person makes him invisible to you. (I blocked Lucius only as an example.)

What happens if you block Lucius Kwok

- You will no longer see this person's content in your stream.
- This person won't be able to comment on your content.
- This person will be removed from your circles.
- This person will still be able to see your public posts.

Lucius Kwok won't receive an email about these changes. You can always unblock this person later.

Cancel   Block Lucius Kwok

Before you click the blue Block button, make sure that you understand the ramifications:

- The blocked person's content won't appear in your stream.
- The blocked person won't be able to comment on anything you post.
- The blocked person is kicked out of any of your circles he or she was in.

The person you blocked will be able to see any of your public posts on Google+ but won't be able to comment on them. Don't worry about offending someone by blocking him or her: Google+ won't notify people about being blocked (though they may figure it out on their own when they can no longer comment on your public posts).

To unblock someone, follow these steps:

1. Click the Circles icon in the Google+ toolbar to go to the circle browser (see Chapter 2).

2. Choose View Blocked from the More Actions menu (**Figure 3.67** on the next page).

All the people you've blocked are listed, along with an Unblock link next to each name (**Figure 3.68**).

Figure 3.67 The More Actions menu in the circle browser allows you to display everyone you've blocked.

Figure 3.68 The blocked list allows you to unblock people.

3.   Click the Unblock link.

4.   Click the blue Done button.

The person is once again able to interact with you fully on Google+ (**Figure 3.69**). Make sure to add the person to some circles, because he was forcibly ejected from all your circles when you blocked him.

Figure 3.69 Because Lucius was removed from all my circles when I blocked him, the unblocked alert includes a handy Add to Circles button.

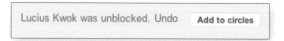

Navigating the Stream

Getting from post to post on the stream is straightforward: Just scroll down.

The most recent content appears at the top, with earlier posts arranged below. An older post might appear back up at the top when someone leaves a new comment on it. If you're a keyboard jockey, you can jump through posts by pressing the J key to go forward post by post and K to go backward.

When a post is selected, a blue line appears on its left side (**Figure 3.70**).

Figure 3.70 The selected post is highlighted.

As you make your way down the stream, you may want to hop to the top so you can access the share box. To jump to the top of the stream quickly, just double-click the black Plus bar. That'll scroll up to the top of the stream automatically.

Filters

I have a bunch of circles composed of people who generally post about the same thing. By default, my stream shows the people I follow jumbled all together, which is fine, but sometimes I just want to see what my Mac People are sharing.

The left column of the stream includes a section called Stream, with a list of all your circles (**Figure 3.71**). As you can see in Figure 3.71, Stream is in red because this isn't just a simple list of circles; it's a list of filters that you can apply to your stream. The active filter—in this case, Stream—is displayed in red.

To see updates from a particular circle, click it in the filter list (**Figure 3.72**).

Figure 3.71 (near right)
Your available stream filters.

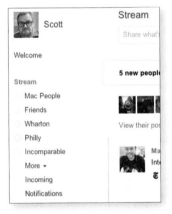

Figure 3.72 (far right)
The stream showing only those posts from people in my Mac People circle.

Incoming

Among the circle-based filters is something called Incoming. Chances are that you don't have a circle called Incoming, so what the heck is it? The Incoming filter shows you things that people who aren't in any of your circles have shared with you. This may mean that they've shared an item with one of their circles that includes you or that they're sharing something directly with you. Either way, it'll show up in the Incoming section of your stream.

An alert is displayed at the top of your stream, displaying the number of people who are sharing things with you, along with their profile pictures (**Figure 3.73**). The alert includes a link to your Incoming stream and an X in the top-right corner to dismiss it.

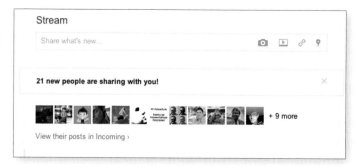

Figure 3.73 People whom you don't follow but who recently shared things with you are shown in this alert.

The Incoming stream looks just like your regular stream except that it's populated by people who aren't in your circles (**Figure 3.74**). Because the Incoming stream is full of folks who aren't in any of your circles, there's a gray bar above each shared item, identifying who shared the item and displaying two buttons: Add to Circles and Ignore.

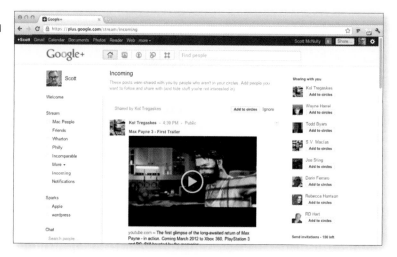

Figure 3.74 The Incoming stream lists all the posts shared with you by people outside your circles.

Ignoring people does a few things:

- Any items they shared with you are removed from the Incoming stream.

- New items they share will not be displayed in your Incoming stream.

- If ignored people mention you in posts, you won't be notified.

If you decide that you want to un-ignore someone, just click the Circles icon in the Google+ toolbar. In the circle browser, choose View Ignored from the More Actions menu. This brings up the list of people you've ignored, with an Un-ignore link displayed next to each. Click the link and then click the Done button to un-ignore someone.

Hangouts

4

Google+ attempts to replicate your real-life social networks with circles. But how can it replicate one of the best aspects of having friends—impromptu hanging out—on the Internet? Google+ has a feature that tries to do just that, cleverly named hangouts.

Hangouts are basically videoconferences that you can start from Google+. Invite people or circles, and folks can join your hangout and shoot the breeze. You can even watch YouTube videos together!

The Lowdown on Hangouts

A few things to know about hangouts:

- Hangouts require the Google voice and video plug-in to work. Download it here: www.google.com/chat/video.

- Each hangout can have a maximum ten participants.

- At 90 minutes, Google+ checks in to make sure that your hangout is still happening. If no one responds, the hangout ends automatically.

- Your computer must have a webcam and a microphone attached to it to audio/video chat.

Now that the ground rules of hangouts have ben established, the rest of this chapter is devoted to showing you how to start and join hangouts for yourself.

 Google+ recently added hangouts with extras. These hangouts offer different features and will be covered in one of the digital updates to this book (see the introduction).

Starting a Hangout

Starting a hangout is very simple:

1. Log in to Google+.

2. Click the green Start a Hangout button in the third column of your stream page (**Figure 4.1**).

3. If you don't have the Google voice and video plug-in installed, you'll be prompted to install it (**Figure 4.2**); click the Install Plugin button, and follow the onscreen instructions.

 After you install the plug-in, you may have to click Start a Hangout again to restart your hangout.

Clicking the Start a Hangout button with the plug-in installed opens the Google Hangouts window (**Figure 4.3**). In the middle of the screen is video from your computer's webcam. As the screen suggests, take this opportunity to make sure that your face can be seen and that your hair is in order.

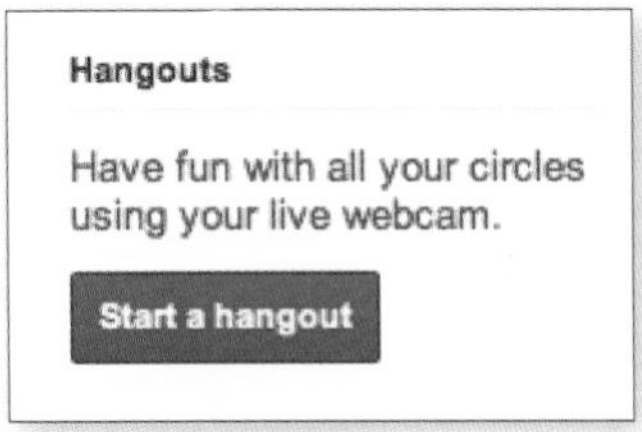

Hangouts

Have fun with all your circles using your live webcam.

Start a hangout

Figure 4.1 (above) The Start a Hangout button.

Figure 4.2 (right) Hangouts require the Google voice and video plug-in. If you don't have it installed, you'll see this prompt.

Figure 4.3 Before you start a hangout, you have a chance to make sure that your video and audio are OK.

4. Familiarize yourself with the buttons along the bottom of the window (**Figure 4.4** on the next page):

- **Mute Video.** This button mutes your video for the rest of the hangout participants.

- **Mute Mic.** The Mute Mic button serves double duty. Click it, and your microphone is muted so that no one can hear what you're saying. When your mic isn't muted, though, your sound level is displayed. The more green bars appear, the louder you are. If no green bars appear, make sure that the Google Hangouts window is using the correct source for your mic (see "Adjusting hangout settings" later in this chapter).

- **Settings.** As you might expect, click this button to see your hangout's settings.

- **Exit.** End your hangout by clicking this button.

Figure 4.4 These four buttons appear before participants join your hangout (and afterward as well).

5. To start your hangout, invite some people to hang out with you.

    You can select some of your circles or individual people. By default, Your Circles is selected (refer to Figure 4.3), which means that anyone who is in one of your circles will be able to join this hangout.

6. Click the green Hang Out button.

    Your hangout is posted to your stream and the streams of the people you invited (**Figure 4.5**). Anyone who wants to hang out with you just clicks the Join This Hangout button.

Figure 4.5 A notice of your hangout is posted to the stream to alert the people you invited to join you.

 You can participate in only one hangout at a time per computer.

Hanging Out

Your hangout is started, and chances are that no one has joined you just yet, so the hangout window displays only your webcam video and the image of a sad, lonely robot to really drive home the point that you're alone (**Figure 4.6**). (Thanks, Google+!)

Figure 4.6 The sad robot reminds you that you're all alone in your hangout.

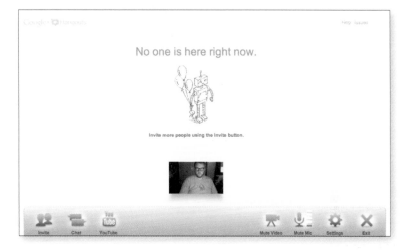

When people start joining your hangout, however, their video feeds are displayed in a line toward the bottom of the window (**Figure 4.7**). The main video window displays the participant who's sending the most noise through his or her microphone at the moment.

Figure 4.7 Hanging out with some friends. Participants are shown at the bottom, and whoever is talking is shown in the center.

You can override this automatic switching for yourself simply by clicking the person whose video feed you want to appear in the main area. That video thumbnail is outlined in green, and that person's video is displayed in the center. Clicking someone else puts him or her in the center. Click a person twice to revert to automatic switching.

Using hangout options

While you're in an active hangout, whether it has ten people in it or one, three new buttons appear at the bottom of the screen (**Figure 4.8**):

- **Invite.** You may want to invite more people to your hangout to get the party started. Click the Invite button, and you can invite more people/circles to your hangout just by clicking the Add Circles or People to Share With link and selecting them (**Figure 4.9**). Click the Invite button, and your hangout adds the new invitees.

Figure 4.8 These buttons appear when people join you in your hangout.

 Keep in mind that everyone in the hangout—not just the person who started the hangout—can invite people to join in.

- **Chat.** In addition to having audio chat, you can click this button to open a text chat (**Figure 4.10**). The chat is also used to record when people join or leave your hangout.

Figure 4.9 Invite people to a hangout by clicking the Invite button.

Figure 4.10 Hangout chat works like any other chat you've ever used. Hangout alerts, such as people joining and leaving, are also displayed here.

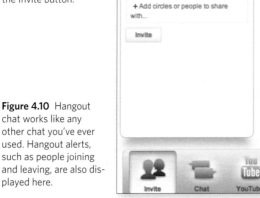

- **YouTube.** Anyone in the hangout can click the YouTube button to bring up YouTube search. Find a video you want to watch, and click Play (**Figure 4.11**). The rest of the people in the hangout get an alert telling them that you're watching a YouTube video and asking whether they want to join in (**Figure 4.12**).

  When you join in on watching a YouTube video, your microphone is automatically muted so that people can hear the video. If you want to talk, click the green Push to Talk button (refer to Figure 4.11), and everyone will hear what you have to say. This is a great way to pretend that you're on *Mystery Science Theater 3000* with your friends from across the country.

  If at any point you want to stop watching YouTube videos, just click the YouTube button again, and you return to the normal hangout interface.

Figure 4.11 Everyone in a hangout can watch the same YouTube video.

Figure 4.12 When someone starts to watch a YouTube video in a hangout, the rest of the participants are alerted so that they can join in (or not).

As you're hanging out, you can mute the other participates, though only at your end. Hover your mouse over a person's video, and some icons appear (**Figure 4.13** on the next page). If you click the green mic/volume-control icon, that person's audio is muted for you.

The red hand icon is for flagging inappropriate behavior in your hangout. Clicking it brings up the Report Abuse screen (**Figure 4.14**). You can pick a reason from the list, and you can even upload a screen shot of the issue (if you took one) to further your case. Click the green Report Abuse button when you're ready, or click Cancel if you clicked the icon by accident.

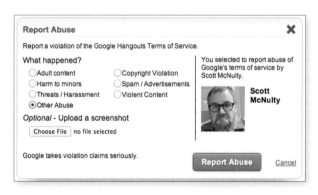

Figure 4.13 (above)
Hovering over someone's video allows you to mute that person or report abusive behavior.

Figure 4.14 (above right)
Choose the reason why you're reporting someone for abuse. You can even include a screen shot. (Just so you know, I didn't do any of those things.)

Adjusting hangout settings

At any time during a hangout, you can click the Settings button to make several adjustments (**Figure 4.15**). The video from your camera is displayed on the right side of the Settings screen. Next to your video are a couple of things to help you troubleshoot your audio. At the top is a microphone level meter. Talk a bit, and if the level goes up and down, your microphone is working. To test your speakers, click the Play the Test Sound link. If you can hear the test tone, you'll be able to hear the other participants in the hangout.

Figure 4.15 Hangout settings include choosing audio and video sources.

There are also three drop-down menus that let you adjust your camera, microphone, and speakers. If you have more than one microphone (such as a laptop with a USB microphone), all of them will be listed in the Microphone menu. Choose the one you want to use, or leave the menu set to Default Device, and the hangout will use whatever microphone you have your operating system set to use by default.

You can toggle two check boxes:

- **Enable Echo Cancellation.** This setting cancels any echoes that may crop up when you have a microphone close to speakers (the usual computer setup).

- **Report Quality Statistics.** The Google+ team is continually tweaking the way that hangouts encode video and audio to further enhance results. If you leave this box checked, you share statistics about the video/audio of your hangout with Google, and Google will use these statistics to make hangouts even better.

Click the green Save button to apply any changes you made in your settings.

Ending a hangout

Ending a hangout is simple: Just click the Exit button in the bottom-right corner of the hangout window. Anyone who joined the hangout can exit whenever he likes, and the hangout will continue. When the hangout owner (the person who started the hangout) clicks Exit, though, the hangout ends for all the participants.

When the hangout ends, the hangout post that appeared in the stream is updated to reflect that fact (**Figure 4.16**). All the people who were in the hangout are listed in the post as well, with links back to their profiles.

Figure 4.16 When your hangout ends, the hangout stream post is updated with a list of the participants.

Scott McNulty · Yesterday 10:33 PM (edited) · Hangout · Public

Scott McNulty hung out with 5 people.

Randy Morton, annie heckenberger, David Snyder, Marisa McClellan, Cecily Kellogg

+1 · Comment · Share

Starting a Hangout from YouTube

You can watch YouTube videos with your friends in hangouts, which is cool. On the flip side, you can start a hangout directly from a YouTube video.

To start a hangout from a YouTube video, follow these steps:

1. Go to a YouTube video.

   For this example, use http://youtu.be/ACNF-XaFfPA.

2. Click the Share button directly below the video.

   In the resulting screen, you see the direct link to the video, an Embed button, and a couple of icons for posting this video to a variety of social networks. All the way to the right of the sharing section are the Hangout icon and a link that reads Start a Google+ Hangout (**Figure 4.17**).

Figure 4.17 Start a Google+ hangout right from a YouTube video by clicking this link.

3. Click the hangout link.

   Now you're starting a hangout just like you would on Google+.

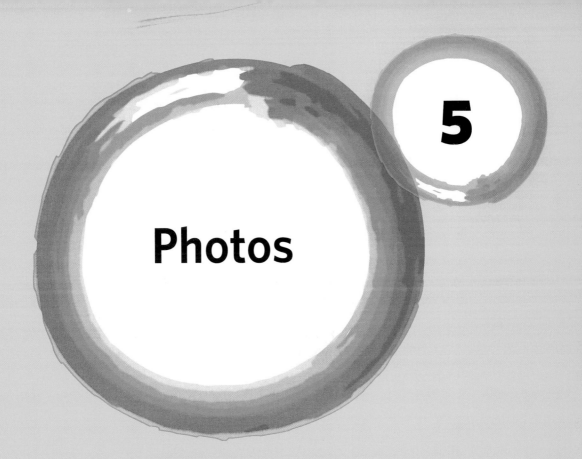

Photos

5

Google+ is a great way to share your pictures with your friends and relatives. You can even share your albums and individual pictures with one person, several people, a circle or two, or everyone in the world.

Some of you may be familiar with Google's other photo-sharing site: Picasa (http://picasa.google.com). Picasa and Google+ photos are linked because you use your Google account to log in to both sites. Photos in your Picasa albums are listed in Google+, and vice versa.

This chapter covers uploading your pictures to Google+, creating and sharing albums, and tagging.

Navigating the Photos Tab

Photos are such a big part of Google+ that they have their own tab. Click Photos in the Plus bar, and you're taken to the Photos tab of Google+ (**Figure 5.1**).

Figure 5.1 The Photos tab.

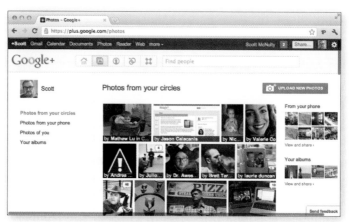

The first thing you see is a big display of all the pictures that people in your circles have uploaded recently. If you click any of those pictures, you'll be taken to that picture's page (more on that in a moment). Each picture has the name of the person who posted it at the bottom, and if there are any comments on the picture, a little white speech bubble with a number appears in the top-right corner. The number corresponds to the number of comments the picture has received.

The left column lists the types of photos you can look at on the Photos tab:

- **Photos from Your Circles.** Take a look at photos from people in your circles (assuming that they've shared any with you).

- **Photos from Your Phone.** I cover this topic in Chapter 7.

- **Photos of You.** If there are any tagged photos with you in them, they show up in this section (**Figure 5.2**). I explain how to tag photos later in this chapter.

- **Your Albums.** Every photo you upload to Google+ ends up in an album. This section lists all your albums.

The right column of the Photos tab has two sections: From Your Phone (if you have a phone with the Android app installed; see Chapter 7) and Your

Albums. Click the View and Share links to check out what photos are listed in each section.

Figure 5.2 Photos of You lists all the photos on Google+ that you're tagged in.

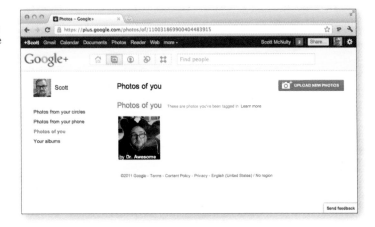

Uploading Photos

Everyone gets 1 GB of free storage for photos (and videos), but there's a very good chance that no matter how many videos and photos you upload, you'll never run afoul of that limit.

Whole classes of photos and videos don't apply to your 1 GB storage:

- The only photos that count against your limit are those larger than 2048 x 2048 pixels.

- Any video less than 15 minutes long doesn't count against the 1 GB limit.

As long as you keep your files below these limits, you can store as many photos/videos on Google+ as you want for free.

You're probably thinking, "Despite these generous parameters, what happens if I *do* go over the 1 GB limit?" If you go over the limit, all photos from that point onward will be automatically resized to 2048 pixels on the longest edge. You'll still be able to upload them; Google+ will just make them a little smaller. Seems fair to me.

 Google will happily sell you more storage space, to be used across all your Google services. Sign in to Google and check out this Web site for pricing: https://accounts. google.com/PurchaseStorage.

You can use a variety of methods to upload photos to Google+. This chapter covers using the Photo tab of Google+. Chapter 7 covers using the Google+ Android app to upload pictures automatically.

Creating an Album

You probably noticed the big red Upload New Photos button on the Google+ Photos tab (**Figure 5.3**). Clicking that button opens the Upload and Share Photos window (**Figure 5.4**). Google+ photos have to be in an album—that's just the way things are—so when upload them, Google+ suggests an album name based on the current date.

Figure 5.3 The Upload New Photos button.

Figure 5.4 Drag photos into the dotted-line box to upload them.

Drag and drop photos (as many as you like) into the dotted-line box to upload them to Google+, or browse your computer for photos by clicking the blue Select Photos from Your Computer button. As the photos are uploaded, Google+ displays a progress bar (**Figure 5.5**).

Figure 5.5 Google+ displays the upload progress.

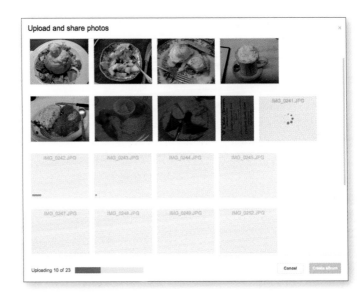

When your photos appear in the uploader, mouse over a photo to see a few options (**Figure 5.6**). The icons, from left to right, do the following:

- Rotate the image counterclockwise.

- Rotate the image clockwise.

- Delete the image.

You can also add a caption in the uploader by clicking Add Caption. This caption appears below the photo in the uploader, in the photo album, and on the photo's individual page.

Figure 5.6 (below) You can do a few things to an uploaded photo in the photo uploader: Rotate the picture, delete it, and add a caption.

As you're waiting for your photos to upload, you may as well change the name of your album. You can either enter a new name or click the Add to an Existing Album link to append these photos to one of your albums. When you click the link, a drop-down menu lists all your albums (**Figure 5.7**). Choose the one you want to add these pictures to, and Google+ takes care of the rest.

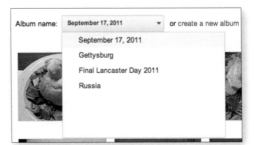

Figure 5.7 (left) Select the album you want to add the uploaded photos to, or create a new album.

After you've either named your album or picked an existing album, click the Create Album button or the Add Photos button to complete the upload.

The album is created (or your photos are added to an album), and Google+ suggests that you share the album by displaying the standard sharing box (**Figure 5.8**). As with anything that you share, you can write a text message (and mention people) and add people/circles to share it with. Click the Share button when you're set, and the album is posted to your stream (**Figure 5.9**)

Figure 5.9 (above)   A shared album in my stream.

Figure 5.8 (above) When you share an album, all the usual options are available.

Viewing Albums

Go to the Photo tabs and click the Your Albums link (refer to Figure 5.1) to see all your albums listed (**Figure 5.10**). Your albums include two that Google+ automatically creates and updates: Photos from Posts and Profile Photos. Both albums contain the photos that the name implies.

Figure 5.10 When you hover your mouse over an album, the photos fan out. Neat.

An icon of a stack of photos with a photo from your album on top represents each of your albums. When you mouse over an album, the stack spreads out a little so you can see more pictures in the album (refer to Figure 5.10). But you don't need to be in the album to see some basic information:

- The name of the album is displayed below each album icon.

- Next to the name is an icon. The globe icon ◎ means that the album is public. The circle with a line through it ⊘ denotes an album that isn't being shared with anyone, and the icon of two people ⁂ means that only certain people/circles can see the album.

- The number of pictures in each album is also displayed.

Click an album to see the photos it contains, as well as to configure and share it (**Figure 5.11**).

Figure 5.11 Click the album to see all the photos in it.

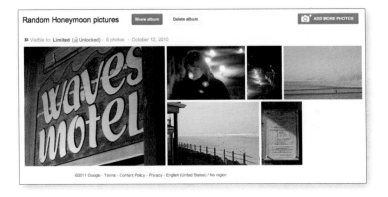

The name of the album is displayed at the top of the page (you can change the title by clicking it and editing away), and next to that are a green Share Album button, a gray Delete Album button, and the red Add More Photos button.

Setting album visibility

The visibility settings are right below the title of the album (refer to Figure 5.11). Click the current visibility level to alter this setting (**Figure 5.12** on the next page). At the moment, only people who have the URL displayed in Figure 5.12 can access this album. To change the visibility to something a little more Google+ friendly, just click the Add More People link, and add some circles/people.

The Anyone with the Link button is a special visibility setting that the Picasa uploader uses.

Figure 5.12 Set an album's visibility by clicking the link next to Visible To.

The visibility settings also include a Lock This Album? check box. Locked albums can't be shared by other people on Google+.

When you're happy with your visibility settings, click Save, and the Share Album box appears (**Figure 5.13**). You can also share albums by clicking the Share Album button at the top of the page. Use this sharing box to post the album to your stream.

Figure 5.13 Sharing an album is just like sharing anything else on Google+.

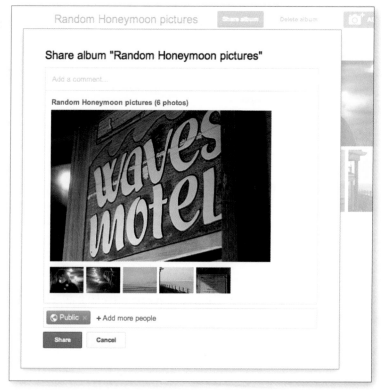

Viewing pictures in an album

When you're looking at one of your Google+ albums, clicking a picture takes you to that picture's lightbox view (**Figure 5.14**). Thumbnails of all the album images are displayed at the bottom of the page. The currently displayed image has a white border to distinguish it from the rest.

Figure 5.14 The lightbox view of a photo.

Clicking the right or left arrow takes you to the next or previous picture in the album. To the right of the picture are the name of the poster, the name of the album the picture is in, and a comment field. Every picture in an album can receive comments, as can the post you shared the album as a whole in.

If your photo has a caption, it's displayed below the photo. Your caption-less photos have an Add a Caption link below them.

Finally, there are two buttons in the bottom-right corner: Add Tag and Actions. Clicking the Actions button reveals a menu of things you can do to the photo (**Figure 5.15** on the next page):

- **Photo Details.** Whenever you take a picture, your camera records a bunch of data about it (depending on the model of camera). This data is called *Exif data*. The Photo Details panel flips your photo around and displays information about it, including some Exif data (**Figure 5.16 on** the next page).

  Exif data can include the location where the picture was taken if your camera has a built-in GPS module (or if you're posting a picture from a smartphone). When the Exif data includes GPS data, a Google Maps tab, pinpointing the location where the photo was taken, is displayed in Photo Details (**Figure 5.17**).

Figure 5.15 (above)
Available actions you can take on a photo in lightbox view.

Figure 5.16 (right)
The Photo Details action shows your photo's Exif data.

Figure 5.17 When a photo has embedded GPS data, a Google map is displayed.

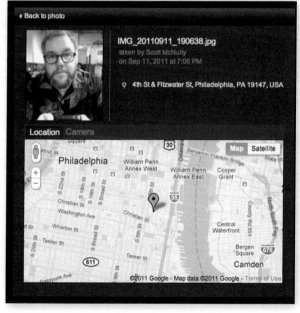

Click Back to Photo to close the Photo Details panel.

- **Rotate Left/Rotate Right.** These actions rotate your photo left and right, respectively.

- **Edit Photo.** Google+ doesn't offer that many tools for editing photos. Clicking Edit Photo reveals six filters that you can apply to the photo in lightbox view. Click the filter you're interested in, and it's applied to the photo. Click another to apply multiple filters to a photo. My wife looks quite mysterious in **Figure 5.18**, thanks to the filters I applied.

Figure 5.18 Google+ offers a few filters for changing the way your photos look.

Click the Undo button to remove filters. Click Done Editing to save your changes, or just close the filter list.

 Google+ knows what filters have been applied to a picture, so you can go back and edit the photo hours or days after the filters have been applied and click the Undo button to remove them.

- **Delete Photo.** Don't want a photo in this album anymore? Delete it!

- **Report or Delete Comments.** People can leave comments on your photos (more on that in the "Commenting on Photos" section later in this chapter), and you have the power to delete any comments left on one of your photos and to report comments if they're out of line.

Tagging Photos

In Google+, *tags* is shorthand for *name tags.* Tags give you a chance to identify who's in your pictures. Google+ sometimes detects that a picture is in fact of a person. It doesn't know who the person is, but it can find the person's face. Why am I mentioning this? Because when you're in the lightbox view of a photo (refer to Figure 5.14), and Google+ has detected a face, all you have to do is hover your mouse over the picture, and a box appears around the person's face with a button labeled Click to Name.

If there's a person in your picture whom Google+ hasn't detected, just click the Add Tag button, and you can drag a square around the person's face (**Figure 5.19**).

No matter which method you use to tag a person, identifying the person in the picture is the same. Type the person's name in the text box that appears (refer to Figure 5.19). Find the name you're looking for, and click it to add it to the photo as a name tag (**Figure 5.20**).

Figure 5.19 (near right)
Tag a photo when someone you know is in it. This is known as a name tag in Google+.

Figure 5.20 (far right)
Now I have a name tag in this photo. My name links to my Google+ profile.

People's names are displayed in the bottom-right corner of the photo's lightbox view (**Figure 5.21**). Click the Remove Tag link to delete the name tag from the photo.

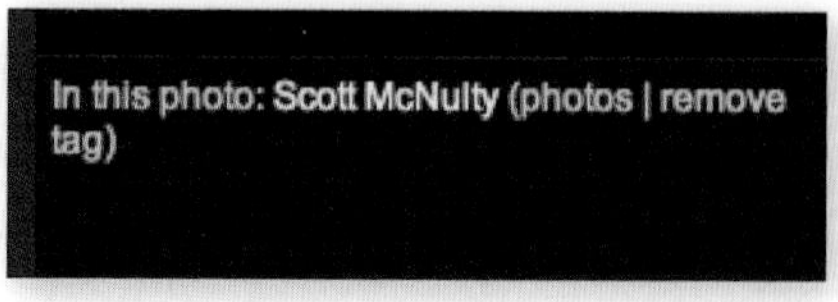

Figure 5.21 Lightbox view displays the name of any tagged person and a link for removing the tag.

In this photo: Scott McNulty (photos | remove tag)

The person you tagged is notified about the tagging and can view the photo and the album to which the photo belongs, even if you haven't shared those items with him or her.

Commenting on Photos

When you're looking at an album, the individual photos that have comments have a little icon with the number of comments they've received (**Figure 5.22**). Click a photo to see it in lightbox view, where all the comments are listed to the right of the photo (**Figure 5.23**). You can read the comments here and also post your own comments, as I'm about to do in Figure 5.23. Just type something and then click the green Post Comment button.

Figure 5.22 Photos in an album that have comments display an icon.

Figure 5.23 Lightbox view displays the comments left on a photo and allows you to leave comments as well.

Interestingly, when someone comments on one of the photos in an album, that picture and the comments appear as a post in the stream of whoever you shared the album and picture with (**Figure 5.24** on the next page). This happens automatically, and it gives people the opportunity not only to read the comment, but also to take part in the conversation (and see your picture).

Figure 5.24 When someone comments on a photo in an album, it shows up in your stream and in the streams of the people you shared the album with.

Who Owns Your Pictures?

One of the biggest worries of professional content creators (photographers, authors, and the like) is copyright. When you upload/share your photos on Google+, who owns them? That's a serious question, and it deserves a serious answer.

Before I give you the answer, I feel that I should point out that I'm not now, nor have I ever been, a practicing lawyer. I've been in a courtroom only twice (both times for jury duty, but I wasn't picked), so I shouldn't be your top choice for legal advice. That said, I've read the terms of service for my Google account, which covers Google+ as well, and I have a handle on what's what. You should read the terms for yourself at www.google.com/accounts/TOS?hl=en&loc=US.

For purposes of this discussion, you're interested in Section 11, titled Content License from You. This section has four subsections, but I'm going to summarize the whole thing in a couple of sentences. When you upload something to Google+, you grant Google a perpetual license to display your pictures. This makes sense, because the whole point of uploading pictures to Google+ is to share them with someone. You remain the copyright holder of the image (assuming that you were the copyright owner before you uploaded the image) and have all the rights that owner status gives you; uploading to Google+ doesn't change them at all. You also grant Google the right to alter your images so that they can appear on different devices (phones) and in different sizes (thumbnails).

Section 11.4 covers Google in case you're uploading someone else's copyrighted material and the copyright holder isn't happy. You agree that you're the copyright holder of everything you upload. (Remember, kids, piracy ain't cool if it doesn't involve a peg leg and a parrot.)

To sum up: You own your pictures, but you allow Google to display them.

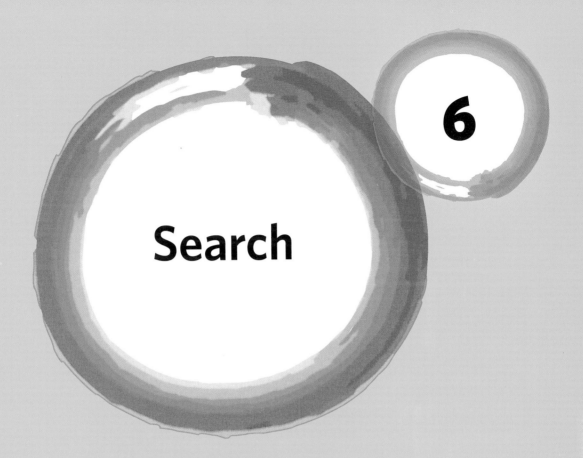

Search

Google has made a name for itself with one thing: search. It stands to reason, then, that you can search Google+ for a variety of things. Not only can you search across all the posts visible to you on Google+ (including all public posts and posts shared with only you or with a circle you're a member of), but you can also search Google+ users. Think a friend from grammar school may be using Google+? Type in his name, and see if he has a profile.

This chapter covers using Google+'s search functionality to find posts and people, as well as saving searches for future use.

Searching Google+

Right at the top of every Google+ page, you'll find the Google+ navigation bar and a Search Google+ box (**Figure 6.1**). You know how to search, don't you? Enter a query and click. But with Google+, you don't have to click. Start typing in the Search box, and Google offers up some suggestions— first people on Google+ who match your query and then general suggestions (**Figure 6.2**). When you click a person in the suggestions list, you're taken to his Google+ profile. Pressing Return or Enter, or clicking one of the additional search suggestions, takes you to the Google+ search results (**Figure 6.3**).

Figure 6.1 The Google+ Search box waits for your searches.

Figure 6.2 People on Google+ are searched first, with Web searches listed second.

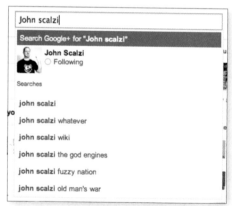

Figure 6.3 shows the results of a Google+ search for author John Scalzi. Because he's actually on Google+, the first thing listed is his profile, with a green button listing the circles I have him in. (If he weren't in any of my circles, that would be a red button labeled Add to Circles.)

If you search for a more common name, chances are that you'll find more than one person on Google+ with that name. In **Figure 6.4**, multiple people are listed at the top.

Figure 6.3 The Everything tab of a Google+ search for John Scalzi.

Figure 6.4 There are multiple Scott McNultys on Google+, and search finds them all.

The search results consist of four tabs across the top:

- **Everything.** This tab is the default tab, listing all the content that you'll find in the rest of the tabs.

- **People.** Listed here are the profiles on Google+ that are relevant to your search (**Figure 6.5**). The search doesn't limit itself to merely matching on name, but also includes the contents of the profile. Therefore, a search for *john scalzi* brings up Ghlaghghee's profile (that's John's cat) because the phrase *John Scalzi* appears in her profile.

Figure 6.5 The People tab shows that search isn't limited to names; profile text is also searched.

You can add people to circles right from the People tab too, which is convenient.

- **Google+ Posts.** One of the key features of Google+ is that everything shared on the service is as public as you want it to be. This means that a search of posts, as shown in the Google+ Posts tab, will be slightly different for everyone (**Figure 6.6**). All public posts that meet your search parameters are included, as are any other posts that were shared with you directly or with a circle that includes you. (All your posts are also visible to you in your own searches, of course.)

  The Google+ post results are sorted by Best Of first, meaning that posts that have lots of comments or shares are listed before other posts that perhaps are more recent but didn't get as much attention from people on Google+. Click the Most Recent link at the top of the search results to see the posts that meet your search criteria in reverse chronological order, with the most recent at the top (**Figure 6.7**).

- **Sparks.** The first three tabs of the Google+ search deal with content from Google+ itself, but what if you're looking for things to share on Google+? Sure, you can share other posts that you find via search, but the Sparks tab is designed to find sharable things (such as Web pages and videos) on the Internet for you.

Figure 6.6 Searching Google+ posts is a good way to see what people are thinking about a subject.

Figure 6.7 Posts in search results are sorted in Best Of order by default.

I'm something of a geek, which I'm sure comes as a shock to you. I'm interested in science fiction, so I searched for *science fiction* and clicked the Sparks tab (**Figure 6.8**). Sparks lists a variety of articles and videos about science fiction that I might find interesting. I can click Share, add a comment, and post a spark to my stream (**Figure 6.9**). Notice that the post is labeled Recommended by Google+.

Figure 6.8 In a search for *science fiction,* the Sparks tab returns links that might be of interest.

Figure 6.9 You can post sparks to your stream to foster conversation.

Keep in mind that Google+ searches are just like Google searches, so you can use the same syntax for more complicated searches. *Sugar AND spice* returns only things with both words *sugar* and *spice* in them, whereas *soup OR salad* returns any posts with either *soup* or *salad* in them.

Saving Searches

Chances are that you'll find yourself doing a few Google+ searches over and over. Whether you're doing a vanity search (searching for your name or perhaps the name of your book about Google+) or searching for the name of a company that you're interested in, typing the terms over and over and clicking Search just isn't an efficient use of your time.

Every Google+ search comes, free of charge, with a Save This Search button (**Figure 6.10**). When you click this button, the search is saved and placed in the saved-searches list in the first column of the Google+ interface, right below your stream filters (**Figure 6.11**). When you click any of the saved searches, the name of the search turns red, and the search is run against Google+.

Deleting a saved search is easy. Just do this:

1. Place your mouse over the saved search you want to delete.

An X appears next to it (**Figure 6.12**).

Figure 6.10 Each search can be saved to your saved-searches list.

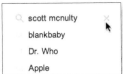

Figure 6.11 Saved searches are displayed below the stream filters.

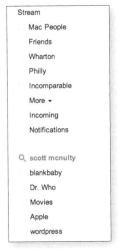

Figure 6.12 Delete a saved search by hovering over it and clicking the X that appears.

2. Click the X.

The saved search is removed from the list.

 Be careful, because there's no confirmation alert; the search is just deleted. It's easy enough to re-create the search, though.

Sharing Searches

Searches have a uniform URL structure in Google+, and the URLs for searches can be emailed to someone else. When that person clicks the search URL, she runs the same search on her Google+ account (which may return different results).

The URL for a search for *Peachpit* (my fine and lovely publisher) is https://plus.google.com/s/peachpit. If you type that in your browser, it performs a Google+ search for *Peachpit,* which you can then add to your saved searches.

Going Mobile

Every time I use a smartphone, I marvel at the fact that this tiny computer I hold in my hand is more powerful than the computers NASA used to get the first men into space. With all this power, it seems only right that you're able to post to Google+ on the go. Not only are native iPhone and Android apps available for Google+, but they also offer some features that you can't find on the Web site.

Now, you may be thinking, "That's great for all those people who have iPhones or Android phones, but I have [insert some other smartphone here]." Worry not, smartphone rebels—Google+ hasn't forgotten about you. If your smartphone has a decent browser, you can access the mobile version of the Google+ Web site.

This chapter covers the Google+ Android and iPhone apps, as well as the mobile Web site.

Google+ Mobile Apps

Google has created free native apps for both Android phones and iPhones. You can find either app at the phone's app store. Alternatively, point your phone's browser to www.google.com/mobile/+, and tap the button that takes you to the Google+ app's page in your phone's app store (**Figure 7.1**).

Figure 7.1 The Google+ mobile page displays a link to the app that's appropriate for your phone.

Both the Android and iPhone apps allow you to do similar things:

- View your stream
- Post pictures
- Comment on people's posts
- Look at your circle's streams
- Join hangouts (with some caveats)
- +1 things

Android App

Android is Google's smartphone operating system, so it stands to reason that a Google+ app is available for it and that it does some interesting things. When you first launch the Google+ Android app, you need to tell it which of your Google accounts you'd like to use. As you see in **Figure 7.2**, I have only one Google account on my phone, so I have only one choice.

Next, you need to decide how Instant Upload will work (**Figure 7.3**). Instant Upload is a feature that's available only for Android. When Instant Upload is enabled, all the pictures and videos you take with your phone are uploaded to a private Google+ album. Then you can share them with folks on Google+ or even save them to your computer.

Figure 7.2 (near right)
Select an account to sign in with on your Android device.

Figure 7.3 (far right)
You can enable or disable Instant Upload. If you change your mind later, you can always change these settings.

The Instant Upload screen gives you three choices:

- **Over Wi-Fi or Mobile Network.** If you choose this option, your media will upload no matter what kind of network you're on.

- **Over Wi-Fi Only.** If you're worried about going over your data plan's quota, select this option. Photos and videos will upload to your private Google+ album only when your phone is on a Wi-Fi network.

- **Disable Instant Upload.** For some people, Instant Upload is awesome; for others, not so much. You can just disable this feature. (Don't worry—you can turn it back on later.)

Tap Continue, and you'll be taken to the main screen of the Google+ app (**Figure 7.4** on the next page). You see all the Google+ sections you know and love, as well as Messenger, which is mobile-only.

Note the red notification alert at the bottom of Figure 7.4. Tap the alert, and you'll see a list of your recent notifications (**Figure 7.5** on the next page). Tap an individual notification to get more information. You can add people to your circles here, open posts that have been commented on, and more.

Figure 7.4 (near right)
The home screen of the
Android app.

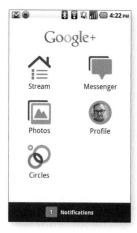

Figure 7.4 (near right)
The home screen of the
Android app.

Figure 7.5 (far right)
Notifications viewed in
the Android app.

Stream

Tap the Stream icon to see stream view, where you can access three different stream views by swiping left and right (**Figure 7.6**). The name of the stream you're currently viewing is centered and bolded at the top of the screen, with other names to the left and right. The first stream view you see is All Circles, which displays everything people have shared with you. Swipe to the right, and you see your Incoming stream. Swipe left (if you're in the All Circles stream), and you're taken to a mobile-app-only stream view: Nearby.

The Nearby stream leverages your phone's GPS system and displays all the Google+ posts that are tagged with a location near you (**Figure 7.7**). Swipe down to scroll through the posts. Only public posts and posts shared with you are listed.

Figure 7.6 (near right)
All your circles' posts
make up the default
stream. Swipe to change
to other views.

Figure 7.7 (far right)
The nearby stream uses
your phone's GPS sys-
tem to display posts
near you.

To see your circle's streams, follow these steps:

1. While you're in the stream screen, press your phone's Menu button to open the menu (**Figure 7.8**).

2. Tap the Manage Views icon.

3. Select the circles that you want to see in the stream by tapping them (**Figure 7.9**).

4. Tap the blue Done button.

   The circles you selected are displayed as views (**Figure 7.10**). Just swipe to change views.

Figure 7.8 (near right)
The stream menu.

Figure 7.9 (far right)
Add stream views by tapping the ones you want to include.

Figure 7.10 The Incomparable stream view has been added.

You can also post to your stream from the app. Figure 7.10 shows the three icons for the different ways you can post to Google+ from the app:

- ☑ : Google+ allows you to append your location to any of your posts, but the mobile app takes this a step further. Tap the check icon to check in to your current location.

  Your phone determines where you are and presents a list of places nearby (**Figure 7.11** on the next page). If you don't see the location you'd like to check in to, you can search for it by using the search field. When you've found your location, tap it to check in (**Figure 7.12** on the next page).

  At the top of the screen, tap to add or remove circles/people you want to share this post with. Type some text. The location is already filled in. Add photos (**Figure 7.13** on the next page) by using your phone's camera to take a picture (the left icon in the Attach Photos section of Figure 7.12) or by choosing up to eight photos from your phone (the right icon in the Attach Photos section of Figure 7.12).

Figure 7.11 (near right)
Both the Android and
iPhone apps allow you
to check into places.

Figure 7.12 (middle right)
The post screen for a
check-in includes a text
note. You can also attach
a photo.

Figure 7.13 (far right)
You can share photos on
your phone.

When you're happy with the post, tap Check In. (This button reads *Post* for the other types of posts.) Your check-in is posted to your stream (**Figure 7.14**).

Figure 7.14 When you
post a check-in to your
stream, it's displayed
with a Google Map of
the location.

In addition to letting you post to the stream and read other posts, the Google+ Android app lets you +1 other posts, share them, and comment on them.

You have several ways to take actions on posts:

- If you long-tap a post in your stream, the Post Actions menu appears (**Figure 7.15**). Tap the action you want to take. If you want to +1 the post, for example, tap +1 This.

- Tap a post to open it.

- To leave a comment, type in the comment box and tap Post.

- If you want to +1 a post, just tap the +1 icon at the top of the screen (**Figure 7.16**). Tapping the three-dots icon brings up a menu of actions (some of which appear only for certain kinds of posts):

  - **Share This Post.** Tap Share This Post, select the people/circles you want to share with, type a message, and tap Post.

Figure 7.15 (near right)
The Post Actions menu.

Figure 7.16 (far right)
When you're viewing a post, you can perform a few actions on it. Additional actions are available for your own posts.

- **Show on Map.** If the post you've selected contains location data, tapping Show on Map displays the location in Google Maps.

- **Delete Post.** Available only for your own posts, this action deletes the post from Google+.

- **Moderate Comments.** Available only for your own posts, this action lets you delete or report comments from the app.

- **Mute.** Available only for other people's posts, this action hides the selected post from your stream.

- **Report Abuse.** Available only for other people's posts, this action lets you report inappropriate posts to Google+ administrators.

Photos

Tap the Photos icon, and you can browse photos from your circles, photos of yourself, all your albums, and photos from your phone (**Figure 7.17**). Tapping each of these icons shows you a list of all the photos in that group. If a photo has comments, a small icon with the number of comments is overlaid (**Figure 7.18**). Tap the photo to read the comments.

Figure 7.17 (near right)
The Photos section lists your albums, photos tagged with your name, photos from your circles, and photos on your phone.

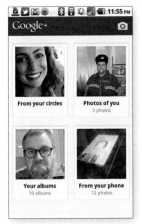

Figure 7.18 (far right)
Photos with comments are denoted with an icon and the number of comments.

Figure 7.19 Actions you can take on your photos.

Tap the icon with three dots to see the photo actions (**Figure 7.19**):

- **Remove Face Tag.** Face tags (see Chapter 5) are displayed in the app, and you can remove your face tag from a photo by tapping this action. (You can remove anyone's tags from your own photos but only your own tag from others' photos.) This action is available only for photos with someone tagged in them.

- **Delete Photo.** This action deletes a photo you uploaded to Google+.

- **Moderate Comments.** If one of your photos has comments on it, you can moderate it with this action.

- **Set As Wallpaper.** This action is available for all the photos shared with you on Google+ (including your own). Tapping this action sets the currently selected picture as your phone's background.

- **Report Abuse.** Tap this action to report other people's pictures as abusive if you believe that they don't comply with Google+'s terms of service.

If you tap the photos from your phone album, all the pictures on your phone are listed. Tap up to eight and then tap the Share button to post them on your stream. As with any posting, you can set the circles/people who can see the post and even add a location.

Tapping the Camera icon in the album list reveals the same actions as tapping the Camera icon does in other parts of the app: Take Photo and Select Photo.

Circles

Tap the Circles icon to see a list of all your circles (**Figure 7.20**). Next to each circle name is the number of people in it. At the top of the screen is an icon of a circle and plus sign. If you tap the icon, the New Circle menu appears (**Figure 7.21**). Type a name, tap Save, and then add people to your newly created circle.

If you aren't in the mood to create new circles, you can tap a circle and view the people inside said circle (**Figure 7.22**). Each person is listed with his or her profile picture, name, and circles.

Tap a person to view his profile, which lists the circles he's in and his most recent post (**Figure 7.23**). The About icon lists all the information he's entered in the About tab of his profile; Posts and Photos list all his posts and photos, respectively.

Figure 7.20 (near right)
The Circles section lists your circles and the number of people in each circle. The bottom tabs allow you to see the list of people in all your circles.

Figure 7.21 (middle right)
You can create new circles from the app. Type a name, and tap Save.

Figure 7.22 (far right)
Need a reminder of who's in one of your circles? Just tap the circle in the Circles list.

You can add a person to or remove a person from circles right from his profile page. Tap the group of circles at the top of his profile page, which brings up your list of circles. Tap to select and deselect circles you want to add him to and remove him from.

At top right is the Messenger icon, which allows you to message with the selected person. (See "Messenger" later in this chapter.)

Pressing the Menu button on your phone brings up the Profile menu (**Figure 7.24**). Block and unblock people here. You can also report this person for abuse if he isn't abiding by the terms of service.

Figure 7.23 (near right)
Tap a person to see his profile. The bottom icons let you see his posts, photos, and About page.

Figure 7.24 (far right)
Press the Menu button on your phone to see these options when you're viewing a person's profile.

Profile

Tapping the Profile icon, not too surprisingly, displays your profile (**Figure 7.25**). Three icons at the bottom of your profile page do the same thing as the three tabs on your profile page on the Google+ Web site.

The only aspect of your profile that you can edit from the Android app is your profile picture. Tap the picture to bring up the Profile Photo menu (**Figure 7.26**). Tap View Profile Photos to see all the pictures you have in your profile picture album, Take Photo to launch the camera so you can take a new profile picture right from your phone, or Choose Photo to select a picture from any of your Google+ albums or pictures on your phone.

After you choose a new profile picture or take a new one, you can move and scale the picture to make sure that people see your beautiful face (**Figure 7.27**). Just pinch and move the picture with your fingers, and tap Choose when you're happy.

Figure 7.25 (near right)
When you're looking at your own profile in the app, you can change your profile photo.

Figure 7.26 (middle right)
The Profile Photo menu.

Figure 7.27 (far right)
Before you set a photo as your profile picture, you can move and scale it.

Hangouts

Hangouts are supported under certain circumstances:

- Mobile hangouts are supposed only in Android 2.3 (Gingerbread) or later.

- Your phone must have a front-facing camera to participate in hangouts.

You can't start a hangout from the app, but you can see all active hangouts and join them (**Figure 7.28**). As you can see in Figure 7.28, Dr. Awesome is hanging out, but because my phone has Android 2.2 on it, I can't join in.

If your phone supports hangouts, the stream post will have a Join button that you can tap (**Figure 7.29**).

Figure 7.28 A hangout in progress, viewed in the mobile app. You must have Android version 2.3 or later to join a hangout.

Figure 7.29 If you have the proper version of Android, you can join a hangout by tapping the Join Hangout button.

Unique Android Features

The Android OS has some features that don't exist elsewhere: the Sharing menu and widgets. The Sharing menu allows different applications to add methods of sharing to your phone. When you're in an app that supports sharing (like the Web browser or the photo gallery), press the Menu button and then tap Share. A list of sharing options appears. When you have the Google+ app installed on your Android phone, Google+ appears as one of the many sharing options (**Figure 7.30**).

Figure 7.30 When you have the Google+ app installed, Google+ appears in the Share Via menu of your phone.

Widgets are little programs that you can display on your phone's home screen. Generally, they're used to quickly display information like the current weather conditions or how many new emails you have in your inbox. The Google+ widget enables to you share right from your home screen (**Figure 7.31**). Tap the share box to share something. The Camera icon lets you quickly launch the Camera app, snap a picture, and post it to Google+. The Album icon (the icon to the right of Camera) takes you right to the From Your Phone section so you can select up to eight photos and share them on Google+. Tap the g+ icon to launch the Google+ app.

Figure 7.31 The Google+ widget.

iPhone App

The Google+ iPhone app, free in Apple's App Store, has nearly every feature that the Android app does, with a strikingly familiar user interface (**Figure 7.32**).

The two apps are so similar that it's easy to list the features that aren't in the iPhone version:

- **Instant Upload.** You can post pictures from your iPhone to Google+, but the process is manual.

- **Google+ widget.** The iPhone doesn't have the concept of widgets, so the Google+ widget isn't available.

Except for those two features, you can do pretty much do everything on Google+ from the comfort of your iPhone: post things, share other people's posts, leave comments, join hangouts (you can't start a hangout on either mobile device), +1 stuff, and view your stream.

Messenger

Messenger makes it possible to send SMS-like messages to anyone, or to any of your circles, on Google+, using the Google+ Android or iPhone app for free.

You can send messages composed of text or send a picture (either one you just took or one that's already on your phone) without having to pay text-messaging fees. Using the Google+ app does require a data plan for your smartphone, of course.

Starting a conversation

To use Messenger, follow these steps:

1. Tap the Messenger icon.

2. In the resulting screen, tap the icon in the top-right corner to compose your first message.

3. Type the name of a person or circle you want to message.

   The app bring up a list of possible matches.

4. Tap the person/circle you're looking for.

5. Repeat steps 3 and 4 until you've added everyone you want to send a message to or you've reached the Messenger limit of 50 people per conversation (**Figure 7.33** on the next page).

6. Type your message in the message field.

7. Tap the Send button when you're done.

   An invitation to join the conversation is sent to each person.

Figure 7.34 on the next page shows a conversation I had with Dr. Awesome and my wife, Marisa. All the participants are listed at the top of the conversation screen. Tap them to see a list of the participants.

Because Marisa doesn't have the Google+ app installed on her phone, her picture has *SMS* displayed on it. Her messages are sent to her as texts.

She can respond to the messages by texting back, and all the participants in the conversation will get her reply. Every time a new message is posted to the conversation, Marisa will get a text. If someone posts a picture to the conversation that won't be texted to Marisa, however, she'll be told to get the Google+ app to enjoy the picture. If at any point Marisa wants to stop getting messages from this conversation, she can just text **STOP**, and no more updates will be sent to her.

Figure 7.33 (near right)
A new conversation in Messenger on the iPhone.

Figure 7.34 (far right)
A conversation, including someone who doesn't have a Google+ app, using the Android app. The iPhone view looks very similar.

Leaving a conversation

If you're in a conversation with more than two people, you may lose interest in what's being talked about. To leave the conversation in the Android app, select the conversation you want to leave, press the phone's Menu button, and tap Leave (**Figure 7.35**). iPhone users, select the conversation; tap the gear icon in the top-right corner of the screen, and tap Leave Conversation (**Figure 7.36**).

Figure 7.35 (near right)
The conversation-menu items for Android.

Figure 7.36 (far right)
The iPhone conversation settings.

When you leave a conversation, you no longer receive new messages, and all the old messages from the conversation are deleted from your phone. (The conversation can go on without you, though.)

Muting a conversation

If you aren't interested in getting new messages but want to hold onto the older messages, it would be better to mute the conversation than to leave it.

Muting leaves you in the conversation but stops the flow of new messages to your phone; it's like a Pause button.

To mute a conversation in Android, select the conversation; press the Menu button; and tap Mute. iPhone users, select the conversation; tap the gear icon; and tap Mute On.

A small "muted" icon appears next to muted conversations in the conversation list. To unmute a conversation, follow the same instructions. (The Mute button in Android is now Unmute; just slide the iPhone Mute button to the Off position.) When you unmute a conversation, all the messages sent during that time are delivered.

While you're in the settings of the conversation, you may notice the Change Name option (**Figure 7.37**), which allows you to name the conversation. Name it whatever you like, but keep in mind that the rest of the people in the conversation will see the name you've assigned.

Figure 7.37 You can name a conversation, but all the participants will see the name.

Sending photos

Sending a picture with Messenger is very easy. In both the iPhone and Android apps, a small Camera icon appears to the left of the text field. Tap it, and you'll get two options: Take Photo and Select Photo (**Figure 7.38**). Tap Take Photo if you want to snap a picture with your phone's camera, and tap Select Photo if you want to send a picture that's already on your phone.

Figure 7.38 You can message a new photo or a photo that's on your phone.

The photo is sent to all the participants in the conversation. Tapping the photo opens it in full-screen mode so you can zoom in and see all the fine details.

Adjusting settings

When you're on the home screen of Google+, press the Menu button on your phone and then tap the Settings icon to alter some things about the app (**Figure 7.39** on the next page).

As you can see in Figure 7.39, the settings are divided into three sections:

- **Google+ Notifications.** By default, the app displays notifications in the systemwide status bar at the top of the screen and vibrates your phone whenever a new notification comes in. You can disable both of these settings with a tap. You can also choose which ringtone, if any, you want to play when you get a notification.

- **Messenger.** I discuss these settings earlier in this chapter.

- **Instant Upload.** Tap the Instant Upload settings to get some more fine-grained settings to fiddle with (**Figure 7.40**). In addition to disabling Instant Upload from here, you can see the current upload status, upload all the existing photos on your phone to your private Web album, and configure how Instant Upload behaves when you're roaming or using battery power.

Figure 7.39 (near right)
The app Settings screen.

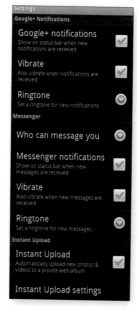

Figure 7.40 (far right)
You can modify your Instant Upload settings, including restricting uploads when you're roaming.

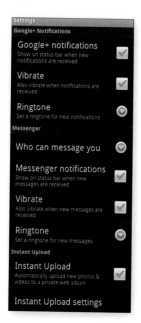

Mobile Web

You don't need a fancy app to use Google+ on your phone. If your phone has a browser and a connection to the Internet, you can just visit m.google.com/plus to experience the Google+ mobile Web site. After signing in, you see your stream (**Figure 7.41**). Scroll down to see more posts, just as you would in the full desktop version of the Web site.

You can flick from side to side or tap the links at the top to cycle through the stream views: Circles, Nearby (if your phone can provide location data to the browser), and Incoming. Tap a post to read it; comment on it; or share, report, or mute it by using the action menus (**Figure 7.42**).

Figure 7.41 (left) The Google+ mobile Web site.

Figure 7.42 (below) The mobile Web site allows you to share, report abuse, and mute posts.

Tap the Home button at the top of the screen to access the other areas of Google+ (**Figure 7.43**). Using the Web, you can share things, repost them, comment, see your streams, and check in.

Figure 7.43 The Home button takes you to this screen, which allows you to see different parts of Google+.

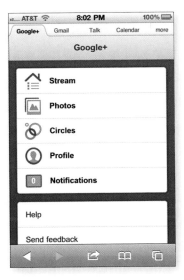

 If your phone doesn't support HTML5, you'll see a very basic mobile Web site. On the basic Web site, the only things you can do are share in your stream and see the nearby stream.

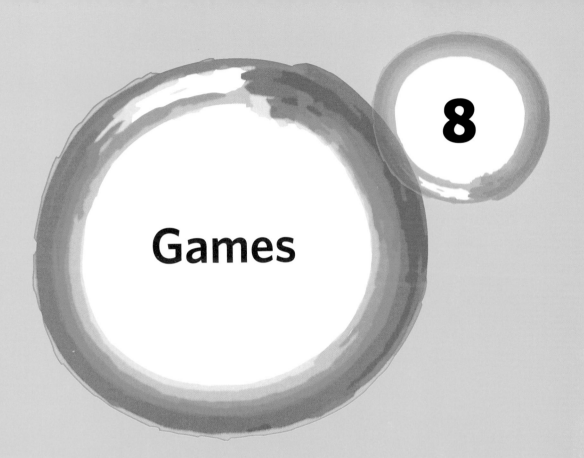

8

Games

It seems these days that no one takes your technology seriously until you can play Angry Birds on it. Google+ satisfies this requirement with the Games tab. Google+ games are browser-based and can't be played on mobile devices (yet). This chapter goes over how to play games on Google+.

Touring the Games Tab

The Games tab features a rotating display of featured games (**Figure 8.1**). Each game has a Play button, a link, and a number of plays (**Figure 8.2**). Click the number-of-plays link, and you'll see all the people in your circles who have played that game (**Figure 8.3**).

Figure 8.1 The featured games on the Google+ Games tab. Why are the birds so angry, anyway?

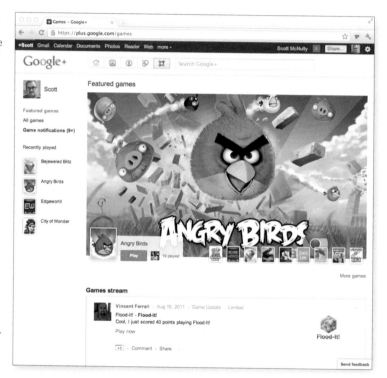

Figure 8.2 (below) The number of people in your circles who have played this game is displayed next to the Play button.

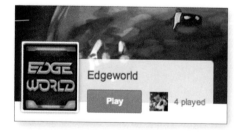

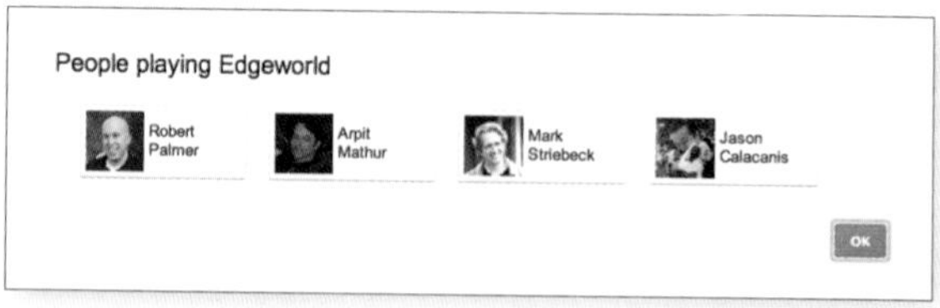

Figure 8.3 (right)
These folks have played Edgeworld.

The left column offers a way to get to the different areas of the Games tab: Featured Games (pictured in Figure 8.1), All Games, and Game Notifications. Click All Games to see the full list of games available (**Figure 8.4**).

Figure 8.4 All the games Google+ has to offer at the moment. Click any of them to play.

Playing

Each game has different rules and ways to play. To launch a game in All Games view, just hover over its icon; a Play button appears (**Figure 8.5**). Click the button, and the game launches in your browser (**Figure 8.6** on the next page). To launch from Featured Games view, just click the icon of the game you want to play.

Figure 8.5 A Play button appears when you mouse over a game's icon.

All Google+ games are played right in the browser; there's no need to install anything on your computer.

The first time you play a game, it requests access to some of your account information (**Figure 8.7**). The permission request details the information that the game wants to access. If you're OK with it, click Allow Access. If not, click No Thanks, and the game won't launch.

Below the game window is a drop-down menu with two actions you can take: Report Abuse and Manage Permissions (**Figure 8.8**). Clicking Manage Permissions takes you to the Authorized Access to Your Google

Account section of your Google account (**Figure 8.9**). You're interested in the Connected Sites, Apps, and Services section at the top. Look for the name of the game you'd like to remove, and click the Revoke Access link next to it. Now that game can no longer access your account in any way until you grant it permission again.

Figure 8.7 All the games ask for permission to access your information on Google+.

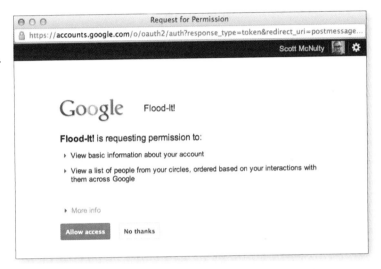

Figure 8.8 The two actions you can perform on games: Report them for abuse and manage their permissions.

Figure 8.9 You can always revoke a game's access.

Sharing

The Games stream (**Figure 8.10**) is composed only of game-related postings. You can post several things from within a game to the Games stream, but the posting always includes a Play Now link that you can click to launch the game in question. Some examples of things you can post from within games are high scores, game updates, and virtual trophies.

Figure 8.10 The Games stream houses all updates related to games.

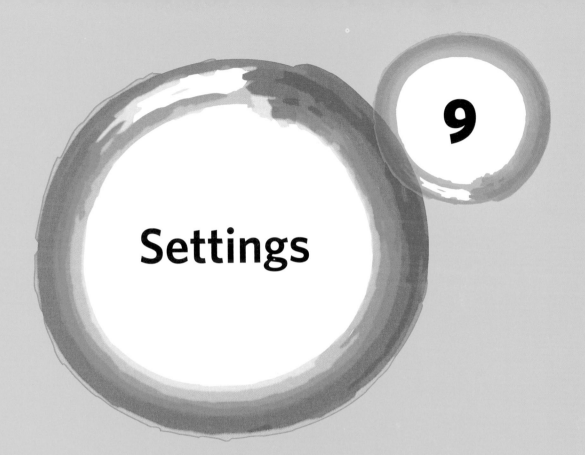

Settings

9

Google+ has several settings that you can personalize. You can tell Google+ what notifications you want to receive, where you want to receive them, and who can message you, and you can even set a privacy level when you +1 non-Google sites. I cover all this, as well as how to export your data from Google+, in this chapter.

Google+ Settings

The first thing you need to know is how to access your Google+ settings:

1. Log in to Google+.

2. Click the gear icon at the far-right end of the black Plus bar at the top of your browser window.

3. In the menu that appears, click the Google+ Settings link (**Figure 9.1**).

   The Google+ tab of your Google Accounts page opens (**Figure 9.2**). The other tabs listed on the left side of the page control different settings in your Google account. I cover connected accounts in Chapter 1, and I talk about the Data Liberation tab later in this chapter.

The Google+ settings are broken into five groups, of sorts, and it makes sense to cover those groups one by one.

Figure 9.1 (above)
Google+ settings.

Figure 9.2 (right)   The Google+ tab of your Google Accounts page.

Delivery preferences

Google+ displays your notifications in the Plus bar and on the Notifications page (more on that later in the chapter), but by default, it also sends email notifications to the address associated with your Google+ account (**Figure 9.3**). Google+ will also happily send you text messages for any of the notifications it sends. (Your normal text-messaging charges apply.) Click the Add Phone Number link and then supply the phone number where you'd like to receive notifications.

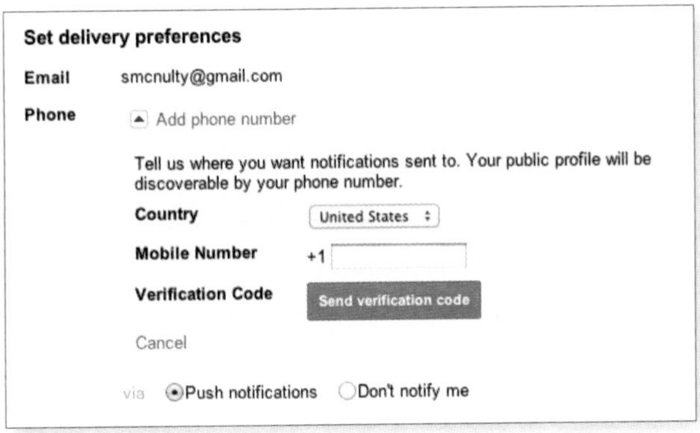

Figure 9.3 Tell Google+ where to send your notifications.

Set delivery preferences

Email   smcnulty@gmail.com

Phone   ▲ Add phone number

Tell us where you want notifications sent to. Your public profile will be discoverable by your phone number.

Country   [United States ◆]

Mobile Number   +1 [   ]

Verification Code   [Send verification code]

Cancel

via ◉ Push notifications   ○ Don't notify me

When you enter a phone number, Google sends you a confirmation code via text message. Enter the verification code and click the Confirm button, and you're good to go.

After a phone number has been added to your Google+ account, you can post via text and get notification texts delivered to your phone. **Figure 9.4** shows your three phone notification options:

Figure 9.4 Adding a phone number lets you get text-message notifications and text posts to Google+.

Phone   +1 215-796-3971
         ▼ Edit phone number
         via ◉ Push notifications   ○ SMS   ○ Don't notify me
         ▲ Add SMS security PIN (optional)
         Security PIN   [   ]   Learn more
         [Save]   Cancel

To start posting updates via SMS, send text to: 33669
By default, SMS posts are shared with everyone in your circles. More sharing options.

- **Push Notifications.** This option is available only when you have the Google+ app installed on your smartphone (see Chapter 7). This option pushes notifications to the app.

- **SMS.** If you want to be notified on your phone, but you don't have the app or don't have an iPhone or Android phone, this option is for you. Google+ will send you a text message with the notifications.

- **Don't Notify Me.** Want your phone to be notification-free? Select this option.

If you're concerned about SMS spoofing (someone other than you sending a text message using your number), set a SMS security PIN by clicking Add SMS Security PIN. When this option is set, only text messages that start with the PIN you've set will be posted.

When you select one of the options, Google+ automatically updates your preferences; there's no need to click Save.

Notifications

You've told Google+ how to notify you, and now you need to decide what you want to get notifications about. The Receive Notifications section allows you to choose which notifications you receive and where they're sent (**Figure 9.5**). The two options for each notification are Email and Phone.

Figure 9.5 Determine which settings should send you email, a text, both, or neither.

 The phone option is available only if you've entered a phone number in the Set Delivery Preferences section.

Simply check a combination of Email/Phone for each Google+ action that results in a notification. You can mix and match. Some actions don't notify you at all (clear both check boxes), others send notifications to both, and some send just emails or SMS messages.

The Messenger options are different from the rest. (Check out Chapter 7 for more about Messenger.) You can choose not to be notified by email, but if you've entered a phone number, you can't disable the phone notifications—which makes sense, because Messenger is all about mobile phones.

You can always see your notifications on the Notifications page of Google+. Click Notifications in the Plus bar, and select View All to be taken to the Notifications page (**Figure 9.6**) All notifications are listed here, though you can click the More menu to filter by type.

Figure 9.6 The Notifications page on the Web can be filtered to show only particular types of notifications.

Google +1

+1ing content, Google's analogue to Facebook's Like feature, is covered in Chapter 3. The +1 setting doesn't have anything to do with the process by which you +1 things; rather, it determines what Google does with that data (**Figure 9.7**).

Figure 9.7 By default, Google tracks which non-Google sites you +1 and uses that data to determine which ads to show you on those sites.

The thing you have to keep in mind whenever you use Google products is that Google is an advertising company that happens to have a search engine and a bunch of other products. Google allows you to connect with your friends and do some pretty amazing things with a variety or products in exchange for information about you. It uses this information to create ever-more-targeted ads that it hopes you'll click (because each click makes Google a little money).

Figure 9.8, on the next page shows the settings that are revealed when you click the Edit link in Figure 9.7. By default, the +1 setting on non-Google sites is On. What does that mean? It means that I agree to let Google use my +1 data (what I've +1ed and shared) to show me things that I may be interested in (that is, ads). You can disable this option, meaning that Google won't use that information to tailor content for you on non-Google sites, and it won't show you things that other people you know have +1ed on the site.

Figure 9.8 If you don't want Google using your +1 data to determine ads, disable it.

Click Save to update your account and then click the gear icon and Google+ Settings to return to the settings page.

Messenger

Messenger (see Chapter 7) is Google+'s answer to the text message. You probably wouldn't want everyone in the world to be able to send you text messages, and the same is true of Messenger messages. This simple setting allows you to determine who can start a conversation with you over Messenger (**Figure 9.9**).

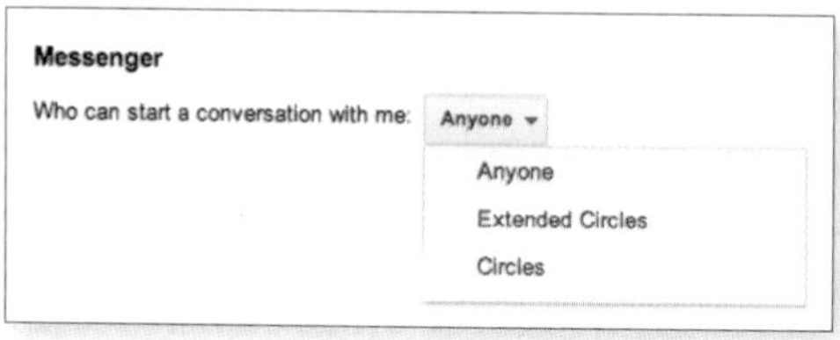

Figure 9.9 You can set who's allowed to message you.

The options are

- **Anyone.** As the name suggests, anyone on Google+ will be able to start a Messenger conversation with you (except those folks you've blocked, of course).

- **Extended Circles.** Only people who are in your circles, or the circles of people in your circles, will be able to message you.

- **Circles.** Only people you've circled will be able to message you.

Photos

The Photos section allows you to change two settings: geolocation and who is allowed to tag you in photos without your permission (**Figure 9.10**).

Figure 9.10 The Photos settings deal with the display of location data and who can tag you without approval.

Most photos nowadays—certainly, those taken with mobile phones—include location data that identifies where they were taken. By default, Google+ displays this information. This isn't a big deal when you're taking pictures of a well-known location, but you may not want everyone to know exactly where you live. Clear this check box, and geolocation won't be displayed unless you explicitly decide to display it on the photo.

As you may know from reading Chapter 5, you can tag people in photos, and they can tag you. By default, everyone in your circles can tag you in pictures without your approval. If you want to allow more people to do this, add them by clicking the Add More People link. You can add any of your circles or individual people in your circles. You can also remove all your circles and not allow anyone to tag you without your approval.

Data Liberation

The final section of settings that I want to make you aware of isn't directly related to Google+, but it's very important. Sitting on the left side of the settings page (refer to Figure 9.2) is a tab called Data Liberation. Google has a lot of information about you, but you can actually export all that information fairly easily and then close your Google account if you like (or just have a local copy of your data for your own use).

Click the Data Liberation link to see your options (**Figure 9.11**). You can click the blue Download Your Data button to download a file that contains all your photos, profile information, contacts, circles, and stream posts (and more) right to your computer.

Figure 9.11 Data Liberation makes it easy to download all your information from Google services.

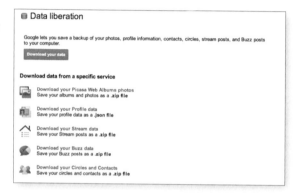

Clicking the blue button takes you to Google Takeout after you enter your password again (**Figure 9.12**). You have a choice of downloading everything by clicking the red Create Archive button or selecting certain services to back up by clicking the Choose Services tab (**Figure 9.13**).

Figure 9.12 You can download everything at once or just from particular services.

Figure 9.13 Click a service to back up your data from it.

No matter which you choose, as soon as you start downloading, Google displays the download progress (**Figure 9.14**). When the file is created, click the blue Download button to download the file to your computer.

Figure 9.14 The download progress. A blue Download button appears when the process finishes.

Backing up your Google data doesn't remove any of your data from the services you backed up. It just creates a copy that you can download to your computer.

Index